# OFF
# THE
# HOOK

# OFF THE HOOK

## Reflections and Recipes from an Old Salt

Roger Fitzgerald   Recipes by Susan Volland

**Ten Speed Press**
Berkeley / Toronto

Some of the recipes in this book include raw eggs, meat, or fish. When these foods are consumed raw, there is always the risk that bacteria, which is killed by proper cooking, may be present. For this reason, when serving these foods raw, always buy certified salmonella-free eggs and the freshest meat and fish available from a reliable grocer, storing them in the refrigerator until they are served. Because of the health risks associated with the consumption of bacteria that can be present in raw eggs, meat, and fish, these foods should not be consumed by infants, small children, pregnant women, the elderly, or any people who may be immunocompromised.

Ten Speed Press
P.O. Box 7123
Berkeley, California 94707
www.tenspeed.com

Distributed in Australia by Simon and Schuster Australia, in Canada by Ten Speed Press Canada, in New Zealand by Southern Publishers Group, in South Africa by Real Books, in Southeast Asia by Berkeley Books, and in the United Kingdom and Europe by Airlift Book Company.

Design by Jeff Puda
Lyrics on page 98 from "The Gooeyduck Song," copyright 1972 by R. Konzak and J. Elfendahl.

Fitzgerald, Roger, 1937-
Off the hook: reflections and recipes from an Old Salt/Roger Fitzgerald; recipes by Susan Volland.
    p. cm.
ISBN 1-58008-340-4 (paper)
    1. Cookery (Seafood) 2. Seafood I. Volland, Susan. II. Title.

TX747.F4985 2002
641.6'92—dc21
2001052521

First printing, 2002
Printed in Canada

1 2 3 4 5 6 7 8 9 10—06 05 04 03 02

# Contents

# Acknowledgments

I am deeply indebted to Peter Redmayne, publisher of *Simplyseafood.com*, for his expert commentary, advice, and unerring accuracy during the preparation of this book. My thanks to John Pappenheimer, former publisher of the *Alaska Fisherman's Journal*—where I hung my "seabag" for many years—for being someone I could always count on for help. And my thanks to Windy Ferges, my editor at Ten Speed Press, for putting up with grumpy old writers.

This book would never have been written without the support of my family and friends, in particular my wife Maura for her steadfast faith that I was doing more than staring out the window, my son Michael, cod fisherman extraordinaire, whose gentle prodding got this project off the ground (and me off my duff!), and my mother, who taught me how to bait a hook and much more.

Finally, I would like to acknowledge all those in the seafood trade who have educated me over the years, particularly the fishermen and fisherwomen who risk their lives at sea to bring wonderful seafood to our plates. They get a bad rap in the press, but the truth is that our fisheries are the most regulated and responsible in the world.

—Roger Fitzgerald

It was amid test samples and photo shoots at the Waterfront Press that Roger and I started swapping fishing tales and recipes. Thank you to everyone who was a part of *Simply Seafood* magazine, specifically Cynthia Nims and Scott Wellsandt whose professional guidance, support, and friendship will always be cherished. Ed Silver, Gwen Hayes, and Noran Volland are appreciated for their hard work and comic relief. My beach-loving family has been a constant source of inspiration. And thank you to my wonderful husband, Jeff Volland, for bringing music to every meal.

—Susan Volland

# Introduction

HOW DID IT ALL START? This thing between man and fish, I mean. Probably when primitive man looked in the water and saw something move, and his stomach growled. "How can I catch it?" he grunted. And when he finally figured it out and caught the fish, what was he to do with it then? Cook it on a stick? Bury it in coals? Serve it *en papillote* with a hint of hollandaise?

I have no idea. I can tell you about my first fish, though. It was in Newport, Rhode Island, circa 1944, casting feathered jigs off a dock for tinker mackerel with my mother . . . suddenly a strike, the fish vibrating through my hands and arms like electricity. . . . And later, seeing it come out of the oven, two perfect fillets crisp and brown with lemon and butter. Or maybe my memory added the butter—we were on strict rations then—but it was an epiphany nonetheless, the first of many, some of which are recounted in this book.

At night, my mother read stories to me, usually set in the South Seas somewhere, diving for black pearls or sunken treasure. *Pearl Lagoon, Lost Lagoon*, a lot of lagoons. And dangers everywhere—cruising sharks, hidden octopus—but the worst of them were the headhunters, their drums getting louder and louder in the distance . . . until I could hardly stand it. If there were no headhunters in the book, Mother "wrote" them in. We longed for adventure. The world was at war, and all we did was collect tinfoil and watch for the mail.

1

Then, in 1948, my father returned from the war and was assigned shore duty in Guantanamo Bay, Cuba. We packed our things and embarked on a Navy supply ship in Charleston, South Carolina—"bound for Cuba." Oh yes, and a younger brother now (who appears in *Off the Hook* as a salmon fisherman). On the fourth day out, the water turned an indigo blue, flying fish skittered off the wake of the ship, porpoises played tag off the bow, my mind forever bent by the beauty of the sea.

My next memory is of Michael Lanigan hitting me with a spit wad while Mr. Stephens was reading *The Lady of the Lake* by Sir Walter Scott. "And deep his midnight lair had made by lone Glen'arty's hazel shade"—*wap!*—right in the neck. Across the aisle I flew, fists flying, the beginning of a long friendship.

We fished together for the next three years. I had a 12-foot skiff that my father built for me with a 7 horsepower Elgin outboard. "No, we won't go outside the base," we'd say, disappearing into a wilderness of mangroves, to places even the Navy didn't know about, fishing for tarpon and snook, spearing *langosta* (spiny lobster) and selling them to the base commissary.

The grandiosity of our adventures grew. One night when we were supposed to be at a movie, we crossed the bay in our skiff to fish for giant cubera snappers at the mouth of the Guantanamo River. I remember we nearly got clobbered on the way across by a seaplane—so close I could read the numbers under the wing. That night I caught a 57-pound cubera snapper, just a few pounds short of the world record. There was a picture of me holding it up in the *Miami Herald*. I had a hard time explaining how I caught it at the movie, but if the gift of my mother was a sense of adventure, the gift of my father was a bit of the blarney.

I had plenty of that. When I was called into the principal's office one day and asked by Dr. Permenter, the principal, if I was going to be an artist when I grew up because all I did was draw pictures in class (of fish, of course), I answered with one eye on the paddle:

"An ichthyologist, sir."

"What's an ichthyologist, son?" He sensed I was putting him on, his eyes shifting toward the paddle that seemed to dominate the office. We all heard about it, all the autographs. . . .

"One who studies the skeletal structure of fish, sir."

It was at about this time that I started writing a column for the *Indian,* the base newspaper, on where and how to catch fish (cooking came later). My career as a fish writer had started, at age 13, although I didn't know it at the time. Then came the bad news that my father was being transferred back to the States, to an ordnance depot in Crane, Indiana.

I hated the place. My parents tried to send me to Culver Military Academy—I had taken to trot-lining catfish and chewing tobacco and talking like my river-bum pals (thank God there was a river at least): "up yonder," "this'n," and "your'n"—but when I turned 17 I did them one better. I enlisted in the Navy. Within six months I was stationed on a submarine in Key West, Florida, operating a good part of the time out of Guantanamo Bay, Cuba—my "alma mater." When we tied up to the ordnance dock (where I used to keep my skiff), Mrs. Burke, my former English teacher, was there waiting. She never lost faith.

It was clear by this time that I had a serious case of "follow your fish," except I kept going back to where I started.

Eventually, I got out of the Navy, got an education, got married, had kids (one of whom supplied the cod in "Cod Chowder: A Vainglorious Pursuit," now captain of a cod ship in the Bering Sea). No, I wasn't an ichthyologist, but an English teacher—at a boys' boarding school in Saxtons River, Vermont. At least for a while. Over the summers, I managed a yacht club on Cape Cod, where I became a bass bum ("Stripers!"), a zombie by day, a lunatic by night, hurling lures into the roaring surf, dragging home fish at all hours of the night.

Life was sweet. I finished my masters degree at Harvard—not bad for a kid who quit high school and joined the Navy—and was working on my doctorate, when one day in Byerly Library, while deciphering an article by Noam Chomsky, I heard the drums. The headhunters! The drums were getting louder. It was either escape or be eaten alive.

So we moved to the West Coast, where I took a job teaching English at Charles Wright Academy in Tacoma, Washington, bought a commercial fishing dory, named her *Shearwater* after my favorite bird, and began commercial fishing over the summers with my son, Michael. Resonances of that experience run throughout these stories. Indeed, fresh "off the hook" was our daily bread: salmon, halibut, lingcod, rockfish, cabezone, flounder . . .

When we arrived back in Tacoma for the fall semester, we were so brown and bleached from the sun (so strong of body and spirit) that people barely recognized us. My wife, who had spent the summer in Paris studying, screamed with delight when she saw us. At least I think it was delight.

In 1976 I bought a bigger boat, a 34-foot combination troller-longliner, and headed for Alaska. It took us two weeks to get there, but we finally did, to Metlakatla, a small Indian village where we fished for halibut and salmon. The next year we bought a seiner and started fishing in Prince William Sound ("Sea Lion Murphy"). My teaching career was behind me now; I was a full-time fisherman.

Life takes tricky turns, as we all know. I had to go to Seattle on an emergency trip to get an engine part, forgot to bring a book, and wrote a story about the ferry trip, about all the folks sleeping on deck, where they were going and why, the woman and her baby in the sleeping bag next to me waking me up in the middle of the night— "Look!"—the Northern Lights dancing in the sky.

Anyway, the story was published in a Portland newspaper. Some tweedy fellow from Back East, at that time a halibut fisherman, read it and offered me a job as a writer for a nonexistent newspaper. Nonexistent writing being my specialty at the time, I accepted. Twenty-five years later I'm still writing for it—the *Alaska Fisherman's Journal.*

But that was only the beginning. The company expanded. We started a magazine called *Seafood Leader,* an international seafood trade publication, and my travels now expanded from Alaska to every major continent in the world—writing about seafood.

My first major trip was to Chile ("The Great White: A Seafood Adventure") during the dictatorship of Augusto Pinochet. I was invited by the government to tour the country's fishing industry, their motive clearly being to export more seafood to the United States. Arriving in Santiago exhausted from the flight, I was immediately escorted into a sleek limo and taken to a conference room filled with military uniforms. The title of my talk, which I didn't know I was giving (I could barely think of my name), was "Yankee Dollars."

Not exactly, but that's what it amounted to. I forget what I said, probably some tips on the benefits of refrigeration, ending with the final words of my publisher, Peter Redmayne: "Tell them you want to taste every kind of seafood they have . . . and all their wines, too." (I didn't want to slight the wine-makers.)

What a feast! Chile is to seafood what Argentina is to beef: 2,700 miles of coastline teeming with fish and shellfish. What things I saw! Salmon being farmed in pens—today, Chile is the second-largest producer of farmed salmon in the world. In Punta Arenas, I saw "Alaska" king crab—*centolla*—being packed and exported to the United States. Sea snails called *"locos"* that were being exported as abalone—which you'd have to be "loco" to believe, but business was booming anyway.

From Chile, I went to Brazil and, over the next 20 years, to almost every country in South America. And so it went: on a plane, off a plane, Saudi Arabia, Thailand ("Bangkok: A Tale of Culinary Intrigue"), Australia ("Mudcrab Madness"), New Zealand, Costa Rica, Mexico ("No-Frills Fish"), South Africa, Ireland, Scotland, England, Norway, Denmark . . . If the stories seem to jump from one place to another, that's just me living out of my suitcase. Or seabag. I never gave up my love of the sea, and everywhere I went I insisted on spending time on a fishing boat to see what the seafood was like when it was fresh from the hook—perfect.

Cherrystone clams on Cape Cod right off the shovel, a squirt of lemon and down they went; blue mussels in Bantry Bay, Ireland, steamed aboard the boat in a teapot ("You want fresh, lad, we'll give you fresh"); dorado (mahimahi) day in and day out as we drifted off Costa Rica trying to fix the engine; sablefish in Cross Sound, Alaska, selected from a deck squirming with them—and into the oven. . . .

What I learned from all these experiences are some very simple truths about seafood that I try to pass on in this book—and have a little fun doing it. (If you don't smile, you won't get it.) A confession of sorts first: I'm not a great seafood chef. But as the best of them will tell you, nine-tenths of it is the quality of the seafood. The other one-tenth is genius—and for that we have Susan Volland, chef extraordinaire and recipe-maker ("Zen and the Art of Recipe Making"), who created the recipes that follow each of these stories.

Most of the stories were originally published in *Simply Seafood,* a consumer magazine we started in 1990. They've been expanded and updated, but I think the fun we had doing them is still there. "Fitz on Fish" was the name of the column. I wrote it on the fly, between Bangkok and Bombay (or wherever), whenever I was back in the office between trips. A photograph, usually of me, went with the column—always a kick. They had me popping out of a pile of fish, draped in animal skins (for "Keep It Primitive"), as a leprechaun for a column I did on the seafood of Ireland (all about Guinness stout)—after which I drove to an Irish pub in full regalia (including a green top hat) and ordered a pint. Said the fellow sitting next to me: "I won't say a thing because I know any man dressed like that has got to be tough."

The joy of seafood, the joy of life—that's what it was all about. The two go together. You don't sit around cracking crab by yourself—and you'll never get away with eating it by yourself. Seafood is not solitary food (like a TV dinner and a video); it's communal, celebrative, and, above all, joyful. I hope some of it rubs off on you as you read these stories.

Good reading and best fishes!

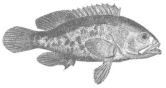

# How Do You Know a Nice Fish when You Meet One?

 AN IMPORTANT QUESTION. In general, I'd say you look for the same qualities in a fish that you would in a friend: clear eyes, healthy skincolor, and no strong body odors. A fish that fits these criteria is a fish worth taking home.

Lest you think this is unscientific, it is precisely the method the Food & Drug Administration (the federal agency that inspects seafood) applies to thousands of tons of fish annually. The FDA calls it the "organoleptic method," a term that sounds like it comes straight from Sigmund Freud, but which means nothing more than "by the senses." Seeing, smelling, touching, and tasting—these are the ways you determine the quality of seafood. No mystery about it.

**SEEING:** Nice fish are never dull or dry; their skin has a sheen to it—like they just popped out of the shower. Your friendly fishmonger will perpetuate this illusion by keeping his seafood moist. This is okay. Dry humor is good; dry fish isn't.

Live clams, oysters, and mussels, if they're not moist and shiny, are dead or dying. The way to check is to tap on their shells. "Anybody home?" If they don't close, they could be a little air sick—or worse.

Look into a fish's eyes. They should look back at you. Some species have a more penetrating gaze than others, but clear eyes are normally an important indicator of freshness. Sunken, dull eyes mean a sad fish, not a happy fish.

Never buy a fish green around the gills. Gills should be a dark, shiny red—never brown or clogged with mucous. In fact, your fishmonger should have removed the gills in the first place because they accelerate spoilage.

Fins shouldn't be too ragged, and there should be no visible signs of abuse—no discoloration of the skin, no cuts or dents in the flesh, and most of the scales should be intact.

Ribs should not be protruding through the belly cavity, a sure sign of a fish gone bad. If you see it, get rid of it.

As to matters of the flesh, fish fillets (steaks, loins, and so on) should have a translucent glow, a shimmering beauty; they should never look dull, dry, or opaque.

If you're buying frozen fish—and more people are—there are two things to watch for: *yellowing,* an indication of rancidity (oxidation of fat) and *crystallization,* a tip-off that the fish has lost some of its moisture (succulence) because it's been subjected to temperature fluctuations. In either case, a tasty fish this is not.

As to the quality of frozen seafood in general, you should know that properly frozen—and particularly frozen-at-sea—seafood is as good as any you can buy. Yes, a fish fresh from the sea can't be beat, but few supermarkets have a dock tied up outside their store. Some so-called fresh fish has been on ice for up to a month before you ever see it. Such a fish is "fresh" in a technical sense only. I won't belabor the point here, but don't be afraid of frozen. Always defrost in your refrigerator, not at room temperature.

**SMELLING:** As I said earlier, a fish should smell like a fish—but not too much like a fish. The difference is between fish and fishy. When a fish, or any seafood, begins to spoil—to smell fishy—it releases a compound called trimethylamine. Consider it a favor. The smell is the alarm that tells you not to eat it. (One reason so many of us are against irradiated seafood is that it smells fine even after it's turned rotten.) Remember, a good fish doesn't have body odor.

**TOUCHING:** This one should be reserved for the privacy of your home. The reason is that touching spreads germs. The more a fish is fondled (poked and squeezed), the faster it spoils. On the other hand, organoleptically speaking, it can help you determine freshness. The flesh should be resilient, springing back after you press it with your fingertip. Saggy flesh is a sign of old flesh. In short, touch it, but don't poke it.

**TASTING:** Virtually all seafood is mild-tasting. I can think of some exceptions, but they're probably not high on your shopping list. Some caviars can curl your taste buds; fermented fish has a taste that's explosive; barnacles can be a bit much for some people—but these are exceptions. Here's the general rule: A fish should taste the way it should smell: mild, with a hint of the sea, never fishy.

Of course, seafood may pass all of our sensory tests and *still* not be seafood that you or I would want to eat, that is, what about environmental pollution?

First of all, you can be sure that the seafood you buy doesn't come from Boston Harbor—unless you catch it yourself. Almost all the incidents you read about people getting sick from eating seafood—highly dramatized by the press—are fish or shellfish taken by recreational fishermen. With few exceptions, the seafood you buy comes from the deep ocean or is farmed under strict sanitary controls (abalone, catfish, clams, mussels, oysters, salmon, tilapia, trout . . . ).

To sum it up, the best defense against mediocre seafood, or worse, is knowledge. And the best way to attain knowledge is to ask questions. The importance of these questions is dealt with in the different chapters of this book, but you have to ask the questions to get the answers. Good fishmongers love fish, and they'll enjoy sharing their knowledge. Maybe you can start out by asking them if they've had any good organoleptic experiences lately? That'll get them on their toes. And that's just where you want them.

# Vodka and Lemon-Cured Salmon

Gravlax is a Scandinavian specialty of cured salmon scented with dill. It is simply preserved with salt and sugar, but never cooked. It is vital for this gravlax-style recipe that you choose the freshest salmon available. This version has been invigorated with lemon zest and a splash of vodka. A citrus-flavored vodka or a classic Scandinavian aquavit would make excellent variations to this recipe. Serve thin slices of the cured salmon with dark rye bread or bagels.

### Serves 8

2 pounds fresh salmon fillet (center cut), skin on, pin bones removed

1 large bunch fresh dill

1/4 cup coarse (kosher) salt

1/4 cup sugar

Grated zest of 2 lemons

1 tablespoon white peppercorns, crushed

1/2 cup vodka

Cut the salmon into two equally sized portions. Roughly chop the dill and mix it with the salt, sugar, lemon zest, and peppercorns.

Sprinkle one-fourth of the salt and sugar mixture into a non-metallic baking dish or casserole. Place one piece of the salmon, skin-side down, onto the mixture in the dish. Sprinkle most of the remaining salt and sugar mixture over the salmon, and then set the other piece of salmon on top, skin-side up. Top with the remaining salt and sugar mixture.

Cover the fish with a piece of plastic wrap and set a flat plate a little larger than the fish on top of the plastic. Weigh the plate down with a few cans of food or other appropriate weights and refrigerate like this for 12 hours or overnight for an initial cure.

Remove the weights and uncover the salmon. Pour on the vodka and then baste the fish well with the pan juices. Put the pieces together like a sandwich again, turn over and re-weight. Cure the fish in the refrigerator for 2 to 3 days total, turning and basting the fish every 12 hours.

When the salmon is firm and cured, scrape off the dill mixture, rinse the salmon, and pat it dry. Thinly slice the salmon and serve with brown bread and butter, or bagels and cream cheese.

Keep the leftover salmon tightly wrapped in the refrigerator for up to two weeks, or in the freezer for up to 3 months.

# Asparagus, Smoked Trout, and Walnut Salad

Seafood alternatives: Smoked Salmon; Bay Shrimp; Cooked, Flaked Fish

Don't let the fleeting asparagus season slip by without trying this. Rare white asparagus is an extra-special treat if you can find it. Smoking trout is an excellent project for experimental cooks and fishermen. If you aren't that inspired, the seafood company Gerard and Dominique sells a smoked trout through its catalog that is exquisite. You can also order from their Web site: www.gdseafoods.com.

### Serves 4

4 heads Belgian endive, cored and sliced

1 pound fresh asparagus, blanched, chilled, and sliced into 1-inch pieces

$1/2$ cup fresh peas, blanched (or thawed frozen peas)

2 tablespoons freshly squeezed lemon juice

1 teaspoon Dijon mustard

1 teaspoon snipped fresh chives

$1/2$ teaspoon salt

$1/4$ teaspoon freshly ground black pepper

$1/4$ cup walnut oil

$1/2$ pound smoked trout, skin and bones removed

$1/2$ cup toasted walnuts

In a large bowl, toss together the endive, asparagus, and peas.

In a small bowl, whisk together the lemon juice, mustard, chives, salt, and pepper. Drizzle in the walnut oil and mix until emulsified.

Toss the salad with the dressing and the trout. Arrange on plates and garnish with the toasted walnuts. Serve immediately.

# Keep It Primitive

CAVEMEN, OF COURSE, were our first barbecue chefs. They burned meat over a fire because they didn't have gas or electricity or microwave ovens. We do it today out of an atavistic longing for the past—seeing in those flickering flames an image of our primordial selves. For some reason we men find this comforting. Things seemed so much simpler then.

The attraction *must* be atavistic because why else would anyone cook outdoors? It's inconvenient. Women know that. We men do it because it's . . . *our thing* . . . and because women want us out of the house.

So we go. It's our chance to commune with our cave-dwelling ancestors—who, like us, suffered the smoke, the elements, the doubters: "When do we eat?" "How much longer?" "I'm starving, Dad!"

Which brings us to the secret of all great outdoor cooking: *anticipation.* A note of uncertainty is essential in bringing the appetite to a savage pitch—ensuring a successful barbecue every time.

Efficiency is beside the point. (Otherwise, we'd be microwaving outdoors—or even better, *indoors.*) A good barbecue, besides salting our appetite with doubt, should give the barbecuer a chance to rise to the occasion—to deliver no matter wind or wet coals, empty lighter-fluid cans or sticky grills. This is not the kitchen, but the backyard, where it's Man Against Mosquito.

To sum it up, barbecuing is good theater, not good cooking. Good cooking is what you do indoors. *Smart* cooking is what you do outdoors.

Selection is the key to success. Most seafood is a breeze to barbecue, but some simple guidelines are in order. Oily, firm-fleshed fish are best. They retain more flavor, don't fall apart on the grill, and the oil dripping on the coals imparts the special outdoor flavor you want.

Some of my favorite species in this category are: king salmon (or any salmon), wahoo, mahimahi, marlin, swordfish, shark, Chilean sea bass, tuna, any member of the mackerel family, halibut (skin-on fillets only), and groupers.

Fragile, lean-fleshed fish like cod, haddock, hake, and flounder are better kept off the grill. You can wrap them in foil and steam them, but that wouldn't be barbecuing.

Skin-on fillets (one to two inches thick) are best because you can put them skin-side down on the grill, making them easier to lift off—and less likely to cause flare-up (that is, less dripping). Keep the fish at least six inches from the coals—out of burning range. Medium heat is best because fish muscle toughens under high heat, especially if the fish is very fresh.

Whole fish—simple but dramatic—are my favorite on the grill, but timing can be tricky. Small whole fish (such as trout) tend to cook too quickly on the outside, too slowly on the inside. Select fish that are at least two to three pounds, and, if necessary, score the sides for greater heat penetration. A fish of more than five pounds should be covered to cook through.

If I had to choose one fish for the barbecue, it would have to be the salmon—a near-perfect fish for grilling. Even larger salmon, up to 10 pounds, cook fairly fast if the grill is covered—and the result is spectacular. Peel away the skin, and you have a feast before your eyes.

Don't limit yourself to fish. Shrimp (head-on if you can find them) are wonderful barbecued on skewers; just a touch of heat is all that's needed. Whole oysters dropped on the grill until they pop open couldn't be easier—or better. Live lobsters or crabs are a snap as well; just make sure you kill them first so they don't join your guests.

No man barbecues alone. Or woman. A barbecue is a social event that centers around food. If it's whole fish you're serving, know something about the fish. What species? Where was it caught? Real food is exciting, and people want to know about it. The life cycle of a salmon would never fit on a food label.

And wear something "atavistic" for the occasion. Animal skins are no longer politically correct, but wear something that will remind your guests that barbecuing is our oldest culinary tradition. And carry a club. You can use it to beat off the mosquitoes.

# Grilled Oysters

The Oysterfest in Shelton, Washington, is an annual community celebration of the oyster. There are shucking contests and booths serving seafood in every imaginable design. But the crowd is always the largest around the grilled oyster booth. There, volunteers barbecue and shuck oysters as fast as they can. A hot, fresh oyster drowned in lemony garlic butter and a splash of Tabasco sauce may just be seafood nirvana. If you can't make it to Washington in October, try duplicating the fun on your home barbecue.

**Serves 6 to 8 as an appetizer**

1 cup butter

4 to 6 cloves garlic, chopped

$1/4$ cup freshly squeezed lemon juice

3 to 4 dozen oysters in the shell

Tabasco sauce

Preheat an outdoor grill.

Melt the butter with the garlic and lemon juice. Keep the butter warm while you are cooking the oysters.

Place the oysters rounded side down on the grill, making sure that there is at least an inch of space between the oysters. Close the lid and cook the oysters just until they loosen their tight seal, about 2 minutes. Remove the oysters from the heat. Wearing heavy gloves, slide an oyster knife into the oyster shell and sever the connecting muscle. Discard the top shell. Slide the knife under the oyster meat to loosen it from the shell. Spoon on some warm garlic-lemon butter and splash with Tabasco sauce. Serve immediately.

# Grilled Whole Striped Bass
# with Indian Spices

Seafood alternatives: Any 1½- to 3-Pound Whole Fish

If you are expecting a crowd, toss a big green salad and fill the grill with these fish for a perfect summer meal. The fresh flavors of cilantro and lime and the exotic spices work perfectly with the sweet taste of the striped bass. If you find yourself without many of the whole spices, go ahead and use a little good-quality curry powder instead.

### Serves 2

½ teaspoon coriander seeds

¼ teaspoon cumin seeds

¼ teaspoon fennel seeds

Pinch of crushed chile flakes

2 cloves garlic, sliced

1 striped bass (approximately 2 pounds)

¼ teaspoon salt

¼ teaspoon freshly ground black pepper

4 slices peeled fresh ginger, about the size of a quarter

1 shallot, sliced

1 cinnamon stick

3 to 4 lime slices

¼ cup cilantro sprigs, loosely packed

Toast the coriander, cumin, fennel, and chile flakes in a small, dry skillet until they are aromatic and start to crackle, about 2½ minutes. Place the spices in a mortar and pestle or blender with the garlic. Pound or blend into a coarse paste.

Wipe the inside and outside of the fish with a paper towel and make a few slashes into each side of the fish for even cooking. Rub the fish with the spice paste and sprinkle with salt and pepper. Stuff with the ginger slices, shallot, cinnamon, lime slices, and cilantro. Bind the fish closed with twine or close the cavity with toothpicks.

Preheat an outdoor grill.

Grill the fish for 7 minutes on each side. Remember that the trickiest part of grilling a whole fish is the ability to *leave it alone* for long enough to char and separate easily from the grilling surface. To turn the fish over easily, simply roll it over with a large spatula. Check the fish for doneness by carefully peeking into the flesh with a fork at the thickest part. It should be just opaque all the way through.

Alternatively, roast the whole fish on a rack in a roasting pan at 500° for 18 to 20 minutes. Serve immediately.

# Greek Swordfish Salad

Seafood alternatives: Tuna, Shrimp, Mako Shark, Halibut

This is a perfect, quick-to-fix dinner. Swordfish is threaded onto rosemary branches or skewers, grilled, and served with vine-ripened tomatoes, onions, and cucumbers fresh from the garden. Start your dinner off with bowls of plump pistachio nuts and an icy glass of ouzo, and you may feel transported to the herb-covered hills of the Greek Islands.

| Serves 4 |
| --- |

**Marinade**

1 lemon

¹/₂ cup olive oil

2 cloves garlic, minced

1 teaspoon chopped fresh rosemary

1 teaspoon chopped fresh oregano or marjoram

¹/₄ teaspoon salt

Freshly ground black pepper

1 pound swordfish, cut into 1-inch cubes

4 large, sturdy rosemary branches stripped of all leaves (or use metal or bamboo skewers)

Juice the lemon into a medium bowl. Cut the rind into chunks and add to the lemon juice. Stir in the olive oil, garlic, rosemary, oregano, salt, and pepper. Add the swordfish pieces, stir well, and let marinate for 1 hour.

Preheat an outdoor grill.

Remove the fish from the marinade and skewer onto the rosemary branches. If the branches are brittle, poke a hole through the fish with a small knife before threading onto the rosemary. Arrange 5 or 6 chunks loosely on each branch. Grill the skewers until the fish is just cooked through, about 3 minutes on each side.

(continued)

(continued from page 17)

## Salad

8 crisp lettuce leaves, such as romaine or green leaf

2 ripe tomatoes, cut into wedges

1 English cucumber, sliced

1/2 red onion, thinly sliced

1/2 cup kalamata or other good black olives

1/2 pound good feta cheese, cut into 4 slabs

## Dressing

1/3 cup extra virgin olive oil

Juice of 1 lemon (about 3 tablespoons)

1 teaspoon chopped fresh oregano or marjoram

1 teaspoon chopped fresh mint

1/4 teaspoon salt

1/4 teaspoon freshly ground black pepper

Meanwhile, assemble the salad. Place 2 lettuce leaves on each plate, then top with tomatoes, cucumber, onion, olives, and feta.

Make the dressing by mixing all of the ingredients together in a small bowl. Drizzle the salad with the dressing and place a cooked swordfish skewer on top of each salad to finish. Serve immediately.

# Skate Scallopini

*"Is it true scallops are sometimes stamped out of shark with a cookie cutter?"*

 I GOT THIS QUESTION ALL THE TIME when I worked for a seafood magazine. Or cut from skate wings (a skate being no more than a stepped-on shark)?

The answer is no. Not these days, anyway. Seafood scams used to be pretty common, but less so since the FDA grew some shark's teeth of its own. The idea of a seafood scam is to take something nearly worthless and with a magic wand (or cookie cutter) turn it into extraordinary profits.

For example, plundering paddlefish from the Mississippi River, divesting them of their roe, then selling the roe in New York or Washington, D.C., as Caspian caviar (for about $50 a nibble). I remember reading a story in the *Wall Street Journal* about it. Seems this fellow in a pink Cadillac would buy the roe from bank fishermen (who referred to him as the "Paddlefish Potentate"), pack it into tiny tins with Russian labels, then sell it at a 1,000-percent profit.

And everyone was happy, which raises the question: If people are willing to pay the price (and love the product), does it really matter? In the case of paddlefish roe, the taste is so similar to sevruga that I'm not sure anyone can tell the difference. And if they could, no doubt there would be some who'd prefer the paddlefish, and I'm sure when the "Potentate" went to prison—which he did—there were those who sorely missed his handiwork.

Same with cookie-cutter scallops. Maybe some liked skate better. Or maybe they appreciated handmade seafood.

I know this much: Making scallops out of skate is no piece of cake. I know because I tried it myself. I used a thorny skate, *R. radiat,* for my experiment. It weighed about 15 pounds and came from Boston. Finding it wasn't easy. Most of our skate is exported to France, where *raie au beurre noir* is a national dish. (In France, they'd rather punch skate out of scallops.) The cookie cutter was supplied by the magazine's food editor.

The experiment led to a number of discoveries, all unpleasant. The first is that a skate is not cookie dough, but rather has the texture of a rubber boot. After several failed attempts to puncture the thorny skate with the cookie cutter, I pounced upon it with all my weight with the cookie cutter thrust forward in the attack position, resulting in a large circle in my chest! Finally, I got a hammer—*wap! wap! wap!*—driving the cookie cutter into the skate wing. At last, I had perforated the thorny skate. I repeated the process *(wap! wap! wap!)* until I came to the conclusion that this was no way to make money.

Then I remembered something about imitation scallops: They're always oversized. It makes economic sense. One big scallop takes half the labor of two little ones. The bigger they get, the more money they make. Back in the 1950s, in the heyday of the whopper scallop, they grew to the size of hockey pucks. When they got that big, they called them "ocean" scallops or "deep-sea" scallops as though it explained their gargantuan size.

A scallop that big would scare you to death if you encountered one in the water. The meat that you eat is only the adductor muscle. If you added shells and a body to some of these "deep-sea" scallops, they'd be a threat to swimmers. I can hear it now: the clapping of the Killer Scallops!

But those days are gone. Not that there aren't a few seafood scams still around. In fact, there's still a problem with oversized scallops, only not the cookie-cutter kind. If you see scallops today that look like they've been on steroids, they're either big scallops (don't rule out that possibility) or they've been soaked in freshwater, an illegal practice called "soaking" (to add weight). You'll know which it is when you cook them, because if they've been soaked, the extra weight will disappear.

This brings up a good point: Never let scallops (oysters or mussels), live or shucked, soak in fresh water or melted ice because they'll get bloated. Leave that to the professionals. But don't worry too much about your scallops. "Bloating" raids on the East Coast have pretty much put an end to the practice.

Adding water to add weight is probably the most common seafood scam these days—as in the practice of injecting water into lobster tails before they're frozen. At, say, $10 a pound, an ounce or two of extra weight per tail will make a big difference on a shipment of several tons. (Commercial buyers, if they're smart, will thaw some sample tails and measure the weight of the water against the weight of the tail.)

The game of shuffling species, an inexpensive one for an expensive one, still goes on but with a great deal more subtlety than in the past. Seafood consumers have gotten much more sophisticated. Mixing up salmon species is still a workable scam. In fact, I saw it on this very day: "Silverbrite" salmon, an alternate name for chum salmon, selling for the same price as silvers, a more expensive salmon. "Silverbrite" or "silver"—very easy to confuse (until you cook them).

What makes it easy for the scammer is salmon all look pretty much the same to the uneducated eye. Your best defense is to learn your salmon. You don't have to go to school, just use your eyes when you shop at the fish market. For example, you'll notice that a chum salmon is never the same bright red color of a silver, sockeye, or king salmon and that a king salmon is always set apart by its much larger size. And so on.

This brings me to another scam, a fairly common one, which is substituting farmed king salmon for wild kings—the latter being much more expensive (and much nicer to eat). Even here it only takes a quick look to catch the difference. Farmed kings are almost always small, usually under five pounds, the flesh much paler than a wild king (and artificially colored at that), and they're all the same size, stacked like cord wood behind the counter.

The best scam I ever saw along these lines was at Seattle's famous Pike Place Market; a big stack of farmed Atlantic salmon were buried in ice with a sign saying "Norwegian Kings!" Now, Norway has had kings, but never king salmon. But they are the world's leading grower of farmed Atlantic salmon, a nice fish but no wild king salmon. Or Norwegian king salmon.

And there's the lighter stuff that really wouldn't qualify as a scam at all. The mahimahi that you order in Hawaii is probably from Costa Rica, nothing wrong with that, but you'll think you're eating a local fish. Or selling frozen for fresh—a yawn really. Dying fish eggs black to sell them as caviar (leaving your mouth looking like an O-ring) is becoming a lost art, really. Just not that many people eating caviar these days, even if it's phony. All pretty mild stuff compared to the good old days of "skate scallopini."

Which is too bad. It was as close as seafood ever got to art—which Aristotle defined as "the imitation of nature."

# Scallop Wontons in Clear Broth

Seafood alternatives: Shrimp, Hake

A bowl of flavorful soup is one of life's great pleasures; add to it these dumplings, which are simple to make, and you have something special. If you prefer to present the wontons as an appetizer, simply steam or boil them, and serve with soy sauce or Chinese black vinegar. Dashi is a clear, flavorful bonito stock widely used in Japan. It is readily available in the States as an instant soup base.

### Serves 6 (36 dumplings)

1 pound scallops, finely chopped

1 egg white, lightly beaten

2 green onions, white part only, very finely chopped

4 water chestnuts, finely minced (optional)

1 tablespoon soy sauce

1 tablespoon medium dry sherry or white wine (optional)

2 teaspoons cornstarch

1 teaspoon sesame oil

1/2 teaspoon minced or grated fresh ginger

1/4 teaspoon sugar

Pinch of salt

Pinch of ground white pepper

To make the scallop filling, stir together the scallops, egg white, green onions, water chestnuts, soy sauce, sherry, cornstarch, sesame oil, ginger, sugar, salt, and pepper. Chill for at least 30 minutes to set up slightly.

To make the dumplings, place 3 or 4 wonton skins on a clean surface and dampen the edges very slightly with a bit of water. Place a teaspoon of the scallop filling in the center of each wonton wrapper. Fold into a triangle, gently pressing out the excess air and sealing the edges. Pull the bottom points of the triangle together and pinch to bind. Arrange the finished wontons on a tray dusted with cornstarch. If you are not using the wontons right away, freeze them in a single layer on the tray until they are solid, and then package them in an airtight container or freezer bag.

(continued)

**Skate Scallopini**

(continued from page 23)

**Cornstarch for dusting**

**1 package wonton skins**

**8 cups dashi, chicken stock, or wonton soup base**

**1/2 pound baby bok choy**

**Sliced green onions for garnish (white and green parts)**

To make the broth, make the dashi according to the manufacturer's directions, or use already prepared chicken stock or wonton soup base.

Blanch the baby bok choy in boiling, salted water until it is just tender, 1 to 2 minutes. Rinse the bok choy under cold water to stop the cooking. Quarter the bok choy lengthwise, removing and discarding any tough leaves or stems.

Simmer the dumplings in the broth until they float, about 2 minutes. Divide the bok choy into 6 serving bowls and ladle the dumplings and broth evenly into the bowls. Garnish with sliced green onions. Serve hot.

# Grilled Scallop and Grape Skewers with Tarragon

Seafood alternatives: Halibut Cheeks, Salmon, Monkfish

Grilling grapes intensifies their flavor. The complex and refined flavor of the grilled grapes and tarragon are perfect with sweet sea scallops.

### Serves 4

2 tablespoons walnut oil or olive oil

1 teaspoon chopped fresh tarragon

16 large sea scallops, (about 1½ pounds)

1 red onion, cut into 8 wedges

1 cup large red seedless grapes

¼ teaspoon salt

Freshly ground black pepper

Preheat an outdoor grill.

If you are using bamboo skewers, soak them in cold water for at least 30 minutes to prevent them from burning.

In a small bowl, combine the walnut oil and tarragon. Set aside.

Use two parallel, thin skewers for each kebab; it makes them much easier to flip. Thread the scallops, onion, and grapes onto the skewers. Nestling the scallops in the natural curve of the onion makes an attractive and flavorful presentation. Brush well with the oil mixture and season with plenty of salt and black pepper. You can make the skewers to this point and keep them in the refrigerator for up to 24 hours.

Grill the skewers until the scallops are lightly colored and just cooked through, about 3 minutes on each side. Brush again with the tarragon flavored oil. Serve immediately.

# Curried Skate with Lentils and Chapatis

Seafood alternatives: Halibut Cheeks, Chilean Sea Bass, Snapper, Rockfish

Skate wings intimidate many cooks, mainly because the fan of cartilage that runs through the center of the sweet meat looks complicated and bony. But you can pan-fry, roast, grill, or steam the fish, just like any other fillet. When the skate is cooked, simply lift the flesh from the "bones" with a flat spatula. Pull the cartilage out and discard it. You can then tear the meat into strips or serve it as a whole fillet. Here, the skate is rubbed with curry, broiled, and served with lentils and sprouts in chapatis (whole wheat Indian flatbread) to make an Indian "taco." Tiny pea sprouts are becoming quite popular in Asian markets and better grocery stores.

| Serves 4 |
|---|

1½ cups lentils

1 cinnamon stick

2 tablespoons butter

1 medium onion, diced

1 teaspoon minced fresh ginger

2 ripe tomatoes, diced

3 tablespoons Madras curry paste
or curry powder

1 cup chicken or vegetable stock

1 teaspoon salt

1 teaspoon freshly ground
black pepper

1½ pounds skate wings

In a medium saucepan, boil the lentils in plenty of salted water with the cinnamon stick until they are just tender, about 10 minutes. Drain.

In a large sauté pan, melt the butter and cook the onion and ginger until they are golden brown, about 10 minutes. Add the lentils, tomatoes, and 1 tablespoon of the curry, and cook 2 to 3 minutes more, stirring regularly. Add the chicken stock and simmer, stirring regularly until the lentils are soft and stewlike, about 30 minutes. Season with ½ teaspoon salt and ½ teaspoon pepper.

1 tablespoon chopped fresh
cilantro

8 small or 4 large chapatis

2 to 3 cups fresh pea sprouts
(or radish sprouts or mixed
field greens)

Lime wedges, for garnish

Preheat the broiler.

Rub the skate wings well with the remaining 2 tablespoons curry and season with the remaining $1/2$ teaspoon each salt and pepper. Broil the skate, turning once until the meat is tender and opaque throughout and loosens from the cartilage, about 15 minutes. Pull the skate from the cartilage in strips, discard the cartilage, and place the skate in a warm serving dish. Sprinkle with the cilantro.

To serve, spoon lentils into a chapati. Top with the skate, pea sprouts, and garnish with a lime wedge. Serve immediately.

**Skate Scallopini**

# Eat, Drink, and Remarry

WELL, I TIED THE KNOT. Sixty-years old, I figured it was about time to settle down. My married friends wanted to have a bachelor party for me, but I reminded them that I've been on one for the last twenty years. They were disappointed. The grass always seems greener on the other side of the fence, and they wanted to share in that one last fling.

So here I am, knee-deep in matrimony. The wedding was held in our backyard followed by a reception at the home of my former publisher, who was happy to see me "settle down." Naturally, it was a seafood extravaganza.

Susan Volland volunteered to do the catering—for which I am very indebted. Not only did she do a magnificent job, she bailed me out of my first marital faux pas. I told my new bride I'd handle the reception. "Don't worry, dear, everything's under control."

Ha!

I figured throw a few fish on the coals, some beer in the cooler—and that would be it. It always worked for my pals. Then people started asking me questions like, "What are your colors?"

I never suspected choosing tablecloths and napkins (not to mention a cake) could be so complicated! Anyway, Susan delegated the details to a caterer, so the two of us could focus on the seafood: I got it; she prepared it. Regional seafood—in our case, from the Pacific Northwest—was the theme: fresh halibut, king salmon, Pacific cod, spot shrimp.

A regional theme is fast, free of complications (once you have the fish), and a lot of fun. Let's say you're from California. A nice troll-caught salmon, either a king or a silver, should top your list (if your party is in the winter, don't be afraid to buy frozen); swordfish (another fish that freezes well); oysters; rock lobster; Dungeness crab; Monterey squid . . . to mention but a few possibilities.

Or, for something really special, how about fresh, farmed abalone? (What could be more "California" than abalone?) There's an abalone farm (called The Abalone Farm, the first such farm in North America) in Cayucos. Talk about simple—one minute on the grill or in a sauté pan (coated with cracker crumbs or crushed nuts) and they're done. As the steaks are small (one to one and a half ounces), they're just right for appetizers. You can use the shells to hold a sauce (*beurre blanc* is recommended) or serve the abalone in them. A beautiful mother-of-pearl, the shells make very nice souvenirs. One thing, though, is these dainty delights are expensive—figure about $5 a bite.

California is a cornucopia of possibilities—somewhat of a paradox, considering it comes as close as anywhere to being fished out. But (partly for that reason) California has become a national leader in farmed seafood, not so much in volume but in variety: rainbow trout, catfish, carp, tilapia, sturgeon, abalone, oysters, mussels—available, for the most part, year-round. Wolfgang Puck is one of aquaculture's biggest advocates in California. I did a story on him some years back, and I was surprised to hear that his favorite fish was farmed California catfish. He cooked one for me at Chinois-on-Maine in Los Angeles, where Whole Sizzling Catfish is a signature dish—deep-fried whiskers and all.

What if you live in Nevada or Montana? Not much to choose from in those "waters." Ah, but modern air transportation makes almost anything possible: Latin America (Chilean sea bass, Mexican grouper, Ecuadoran shrimp . . .); Hawaii (mahimahi, opakapaka, ono . . .); and so on. Hawaii is a good one because you can do the music, the grass skirts . . . wherever your madness leads you. If there's an international airport within reach, the possibilities are virtually unlimited.

But how do you order all this seafood? Your local fishmonger will have to special order it for you—or you can turn to the Internet. Seafood mail order is becoming big business. Legal Seafoods in Boston, for example, can ship you a New England clambake, but brace yourself for the postage.

Serve the best seafood you can find, and if that means fudging a bit who cares? For example, we used golden crab instead of local crab because we could get it fresh—and because it was a wedding gift from a salty friend in Florida.

Hot or cold? We mixed it up. We served the halibut and salmon hot from an outdoor grill (marinated in an ambrosial brew concocted by Susan). The shrimp and golden crab (sections) were served icy cold from a skiff Susan borrowed from her husband and filled with ice. (I should mention that it was summer, but warm—even for Seattle.) Cod ceviche was our only seafood appetizer, served cold on tostada shells with chopped onions, tomatoes, and cilantro—a very big hit. Rounding it out was fresh local corn (grilled), cold melon, beer, lemonade, and wine.

Picking out the wine was a party in itself. Two friends of ours, John Altmann and Simone Oliver, told their wine-tasting club about our upcoming seafood reception, and the club took it upon itself to help us select the wines. This led to several dinners and wine tastings (the details of which are rather blurred in my memory), but it was finally narrowed down to two (both less than ten dollars a bottle): a Badger Mountain sevé and a Willow Crest Pinot Noir. Yes, the rule is white wine with fish, but pinots pair very well with sturdier seafood such as salmon, Chilean sea bass, sablefish, even oysters. The main thing is to avoid anything sweet: Rieslings, Gewürztraminers, berry wines of any kind. I prefer the whites because they're served cold—very nice on a hot day, especially with seafood served hot from the grill.

All in all, our fare was very plain compared to the fancy menus I reviewed from different caterers—dainty canapés and exotic tidbits (priced by the bite) that wouldn't do at all for my salty friends.

On the other hand, simple seafood had me feeling a little insecure. My bride's side of the guest list were country folk, not accustomed to eating critters with fins and claws. How would they react to the food?

Never underestimate the power to please of a simple piece of fish properly prepared! People swore they had never tasted better food. At the end of the reception, as our guests were leaving, we gave away packets of what was left—a piece of uncooked halibut, some spot shrimp, a crab section . . . and I'm still hearing reports about how good it was, how they prepared it, what fun they had doing it.

Remember, you don't have to be a great chef to have a wonderful seafood party. (And you don't have to get married, either.) Great chefs make ordinary food taste extraordinary, but *smart* chefs serve extraordinary food and take all the credit.

# Ceviche Tostadas

Seafood alternatives: Scallops, Snapper

When fish is perfectly fresh, it is almost a shame to cook it. There are versions of citrus "cooked" fish such as this in many nations. This one is inspired by a classic Mexican dish. It is made with lots of jalapeño peppers and orange juice for extra flavor. Try making mini tostadas on round corn chips for your next party.

### Serves 4

1 pound fresh cod

$^1/_2$ cup freshly squeezed lime juice

1 whole finely diced jalapeño (use less for a milder recipe, substitute serranos for spicier results) plus 1 tablespoon finely diced jalapeño or serrano pepper, seeded

$^1/_2$ teaspoon salt

$^1/_4$ teaspoon freshly ground black pepper

$^1/_2$ cup freshly squeezed orange juice

$^1/_4$ cup finely diced red onion

2 tablespoons extra virgin olive oil

Chop the cod into a fine dice. Toss with the lime juice, the 1 tablespoon finely diced jalapeño, salt, and pepper and let marinate in the refrigerator, stirring occasionally for at least 4 hours until the fish has turned completely opaque and has the texture throughout of cooked fish.

To make the ceviche, drain the fish well. Toss the "cooked" fish with the orange juice, red onion, olive oil, cilantro, orange zest, the 1 whole finely diced jalapeño, and additional salt and pepper if needed.

2 tablespoons chopped fresh
cilantro

1 tablespoon finely grated
orange zest

4 cups thinly sliced fresh lettuce

8 ready-made tostada shells
(or fresh corn tortillas fried
crisp in oil)

1 cup diced tomato

1 ripe avocado, peeled, pitted,
and sliced

Salsa or hot sauce for topping

To make the tostadas, divide the lettuce evenly over the tostada shells. Spoon about 2 tablespoons of the ceviche onto the lettuce and garnish with diced tomato and slices of avocado. Top with salsa or hot sauce if desired. Serve immediately.

# Lemony Crab Mousse

Seafood alternatives: Cooked, Flaked Whitefish or Salmon; Cooked Scallops or Shrimp; Cooked Minced Clams

This crab mousse is a bright, elegant, and economical way to serve top-quality seafood to a crowd. Make it the day before for the best texture and flavor. Use a fluted mold for an especially nice presentation. I like to serve this dish with small English water crackers.

**Serves 25 as an appetizer**

1/4 cup dry sherry or white wine

1 envelope unflavored gelatin

1 pound cream cheese, at room temperature

2 tablespoons horseradish

1 clove garlic, minced or pressed

1 teaspoon Dijon mustard

1 pound crabmeat, picked over to remove any bits of shell or membrane

1/2 cup chopped fresh cilantro

Zest and juice of 1 lemon

1 jalapeño pepper, seeded and finely chopped

3 egg whites

Crackers, for garnish

Cucumber slices, for garnish

Belgian endive leaves, for garnish

Lightly oil or line with plastic wrap a 4-cup mold.

Pour the sherry into a small bowl or ramekin and sprinkle the gelatin over it. Let the gelatin absorb the sherry and soften for 5 minutes. Place the ramekin in a shallow pan of hot water to gently melt. Set aside while assembling remaining ingredients.

In the bowl of a heavy-duty mixer or food processor, combine the cream cheese, horseradish, garlic, and mustard, and mix until smooth, scraping the sides of the bowl often. Fold in the crab, cilantro, lemon juice and zest, and jalapeño. Pour the liquefied gelatin into the mixture and stir well.

Beat the egg whites until they form soft peaks. Fold the egg whites into the crab and cheese mixture. Pour the mixture into the prepared mold. Cover with plastic wrap and chill for at least 4 hours or overnight.

Unmold the mousse onto a serving platter, garnish with crackers, cucumber slices, and Belgian endive leaves.

# Shrimp Boil

Seafood alternatives: Crab, Crawfish

There are lots of great shrimp and crab boil seasoning mixes on the market. For a change of pace, mix up a batch made just to your taste.

### Serves 8 to 10

1 tablespoon mustard seeds

1/2 teaspoon coriander seeds

1/2 teaspoon whole allspice

1/2 teaspoon dill seed

1/4 teaspoon whole cloves

1 teaspoon crushed red pepper flakes

2 bay leaves, crumbled

4 cloves garlic

1 onion, halved

1 lemon, sliced

2 tablespoons salt

1 teaspoon ground cayenne pepper

12 ounces beer

3 to 5 pounds shrimp in shells

Combine the mustard, coriander, allspice, dill seed, cloves, red pepper flakes, and bay leaves in a small bowl and mix well. Place the mixture in a muslin bag. Or, place the spices in a square of cheesecloth, draw up the corners, and secure with kitchen twine. Add this bag to a large pot of boiling water, with the garlic, onion, lemon, salt, and cayenne to taste, and boil for about 15 minutes before adding the beer. Cook the shrimp in the boiling liquid just until the shrimp curl and turn pink. Discard the cooking liquid. Lift out and serve hot or pour into a bucket of ice to cool quickly. If not serving immediately, keep refrigerated until ready to eat.

# 'Dem Bones

 SOME DIAGRAMS OF FISH BONES, *what a great idea,* I thought. How many people really know what lies beneath the skin of a fish? Not many—and some who do would just as soon forget. The idea is to know where the bones are *before* you eat a fish (to discover them otherwise is a problem).

So off I went to find some good diagrams of 'dem bones—or, as some would put it, "'dem damn bones."

You'd think this would be easy enough. Just find an ichthyologist, a specialist in the study of fish, call him, get the diagrams, have a beer. That was my idea.

But finding 'dem diagrams escalated from an idea to a quest. I was beginning to feel like Indiana Bones searching for the Lost Diagrams.

I called the Harvard Museum of Comparative Zoology. They didn't have any diagrams. I called the Smithsonian, no diagrams. I called various federal agencies, including the National Marine Fisheries Service. They had them, but they were useless. All I wanted were a few drawings of bare bones—something that would be useful to people like ourselves.

Then I thought of Steve Connolly, Boston's Codfather. Someone from the seafood industry—that was it! Someone who could get to the marrow of the matter, so to speak. These ichthyologists didn't even know what a pin bone was. Connolly teaches fish in his own fish school. He'd know.

"Hey, Steve, got some diagrams of 'dem bones?"

"Damn bones is right! Sorry, I can't help you, kid. I got a buyer on the other line . . ."

Finally, I contacted Sandra Noel, a fish artist and marine biologist. If you can't get it done, find a woman—that's how it works around my office, anyway. She promised to help.

Meanwhile, I continued my quest into the world of fish bones. I visited Chris Reardan, manager of a seafood processing plant in Seattle, who gave me some pointers on pin bones. Pin bones are the bane of processors, as well as consumers: a fish's best revenge after you catch it. Either you tweeze them out, one at a time, with a pair of needle-nose pliers, or you have to cut them out. The latter wastes a lot of fish, increasing the cost of production.

Either way, pin bones are expensive—higher labor costs on the one hand, lower recovery on the other. And either way, no guarantee you got them all.

Pin bones are the peskiest of bones because they are often unattached, lurking loosely between the muscle flakes of the fish, waiting to stick in your craw.

Personally, pin bones don't bother me very much. They're relatively soft and "friendly." In earlier times (when men were men), pin bones were chewed and swallowed without a second thought. But today we are living in an ichthyophobic age.

I got on the fish-bone hot line and got the name of an ichthyologist at the University of Washington College of Fisheries—Dr. L. S. Smith. "Why do fish have bones?" I asked.

Let me digress here for a moment to give you a hint about talking to ichthyologists. "Why" questions drive them crazy. The same with biologists, who will hang up immediately. Ichthyologists won't. You'll hear them breathing hard on the other end. They want to hang up, but they're lonely. They hunger to talk about 'dem bones, but ask them why, and they'll always give you the same answer. "I don't know."

"I don't know," said Dr. Smith, and he spent the rest of the afternoon telling me why he didn't know why.

"Are you sure I'm not taking you away from your work?"

"No, no, no."

Dr. Smith said the bones of a fish function like a "bent bow," propelling the body of the fish (the arrow) through the water. Some fish rely on their fins to propel them, the stiff-bodied bottom fishes like snappers and groupers, while others use their bodies almost entirely—eels, for example.

I had never thought of this before. I pictured the tunas, their spines like longbows thrusting them through the water. Tunas are rover-predators; monkfish are lie-and-wait predators . . . and so on. There are surface-oriented fish that go either way. Different bones for different zones—there was no end to it. Fish that swim forward, fish that swim backward, fish that walk over land, fish that fly. . . .

None of this was possible without 'dem bones. Bones make up the fins of fish, the "wings" of the watery world. . . . A halo of light began to appear on 'dem bones.

My next stop was the laboratory of Jean Dunn, another ichthyologist. I spent the morning examining slides of juvenile fish. You can't imagine how intricate—how elegant—is the architecture of a simple fish! The slides were treated with dye to distinguish cartilage from developing bone, adding brilliance to a mind-boggling complexity of form.

Sharks, I learned, never ossify (meaning their cartilage never turns to bone); they're all cartilage, no bone. Same with sturgeon. Dr. Dunn explained that such species are still primitive. Every species is in a state of revision—evolution—which explains such bones as the predorsals, the small spines that you see just before the dorsal fin, to which bones were once attached (but now lie hidden in the flesh). Evolution, Dr. Dunn pointed out, is always toward greater simplification. In a million years, they'll be gone, but in the meantime watch out!

Looking through the microscope, listening to him talk, I began to realize that 'dem bones were . . . *beautiful.* Suddenly, the light in the laboratory increased to a blinding intensity—until I had to cover my eyes. I knew then that I was getting closer to the Lost Diagrams.

I hurried back to my office muttering to myself, *'dem bones, 'dem bones, 'dem bones* . . . arriving just in time to catch the phone ringing. It was Sandra Noel.

"I've been talking to Dr. Donaldson . . ." Lauren Donaldson, internationally famous inventor of the Donaldson trout.

"What did he say?" I could hardly wait for the answer.

"He said x-ray the fish, then copy the x-rays."

The light was blinding!

Thus endeth the quest for 'dem bones.

# Swordfish Piccata

Seafood alternatives: Sole, Albacore Tuna

Chicken or veal quickly fried with butter and capers is an Italian restaurant staple and an easy dish to cook at home. But once you try swordfish, thinly sliced, breaded, and cooked in this manner, you may never go back. This dish has even turned swordfish skeptics into fans, and kids love it.

### Serves 4

4 (4 to 6-ounce) swordfish steaks

1/2 teaspoon salt plus more to taste

1/4 teaspoon freshly ground black pepper plus more to taste

1/4 cup flour

2 eggs, beaten

1 1/2 cups Italian-style bread crumbs

4 to 6 tablespoons butter

1/4 cup dry white wine

2 tablespoons freshly squeezed lemon juice

1/4 cup capers, rinsed and drained

1 tablespoon chopped fresh parsley

Trim away any skin, fat, or bloodline from the swordfish. Use long strokes of a long, very sharp knife to slice the fish into 1/4-inch-thick scallopini. Press down on the fish with your free hand to maintain an even density and so you can feel where the knife is. Place the scallopini between pieces of plastic wrap or waxed paper and pound with a flat mallet or the bottom of a small heavy pan for thinner, flatter pieces.

Season the swordfish with 1/2 teaspoon salt and 1/4 teaspoon pepper. Place the flour, eggs, and bread crumbs in three separate shallow dishes. Coat each piece of swordfish in the flour and tap gently to remove any excess. Dip both sides in the egg, and then coat with the bread crumbs.

In a large skillet, melt 1 tablespoon of the butter over medium-high heat. When it is hot, fry the scallopini a few at a time in the butter until they are golden brown and tender, about 1 minute per side. Remove to a platter and keep warm while frying the other pieces. Add more butter to the pan as needed.

When all of the fish is cooked, pour the wine into the skillet and boil to reduce by half, gently dissolving any brown bits that are stuck to the bottom of the pan. Whisk in the remaining butter and stir in the lemon juice, capers, and parsley, then season the sauce with salt and pepper to taste. Pour the sauce over the fish. Serve immediately.

# Monkfish Pot Roast

Seafood alternatives: Sturgeon, Chilean Sea Bass, Skate

A good pot roast is made from a tough piece of meat that needs long, slow cooking to tenderize it. Because there aren't any varieties of seafood that require such treatment, we will cheat a little. After the fish is browned, the vegetables are slowly cooked in the oven in a flavorful broth and the fish is added later. Choose nice, thick monkfish tails for best results. If the monkfish has not been trimmed of the slick purplish membrane, simply remove it with a sharp knife.

## Serves 4

1 1/2 pounds cleaned monkfish (try to find the thickest piece available)

1 teaspoon salt

1/4 teaspoon freshly ground black pepper plus more to taste

3 tablespoons flour

3 tablespoons olive or vegetable oil

1 sweet onion, cut into 8 wedges

2 medium carrots, peeled and cut into chunks

8 small red potatoes, quartered

1 teaspoon sugar

2 tablespoons white wine vinegar

Preheat the oven to 325°.

Season the fish with 1/2 teaspoon salt and pepper to taste, and dredge in the flour. Pat off the excess but reserve it.

Heat the oil in a Dutch oven over medium-high heat and brown the fish on all sides. Remove the fish to a platter and refrigerate. In the same Dutch oven, cook the onion, carrots, and potatoes until they start to caramelize, about 8 minutes. Add the sugar, stir well, and cook the vegetables 2 minutes more to a nice brown. Sprinkle in the reserved flour and stir to mix. Pour in the vinegar. Add the stock, sage, thyme, and bay leaf, and season with 1/4 teaspoon salt and 1/2 teaspoon pepper. Bring the liquid to a boil, cover, and bake in the preheated oven for 30 minutes until the potatoes are almost tender.

(continued)

(continued from page 41)

1¹/₂ cups chicken, fish,
or vegetable broth

1¹/₂ teaspoons chopped fresh
sage (or ¹/₂ teaspoon dried)

1 sprig thyme

1 bay leaf

Place the fish on top of the vegetables. Cover and braise for 12 to 15 minutes, until the fish is cooked through and the vegetables are tender.

Transfer the monkfish to a cutting board and cut it into 1-inch-thick slices. Lift out the vegetables and arrange on a warm serving platter. Discard the thyme and bay leaf. Place the slices of fish on the vegetables and moisten with the sauce. Serve the remaining sauce alongside.

# Masa-Crusted Catfish with Red Chile Sauce

Seafood alternatives: Shrimp, Oysters, Tilapia

Catfish rolled in cornmeal and fried is a classic preparation that can hardly be improved upon. But for variety, try rolling the fish in masa harina, and then serving the crisp, golden fish with this slightly sweet and robust red chile sauce. Masa harina, also known simply as masa, is the flour used for making corn tortillas. It is available at many supermarkets and ethnic markets. For a thick crust, dip the fish in flour and then beaten egg before dredging in the masa.

## Serves 6

### Sauce

3 ancho chiles, stemmed and seeded

$1/2$ cup plus 2 tablespoons olive oil

2 cloves garlic, sliced

1 cup sliced onion

2 teaspoons cumin

1 (14.5-ounce) can diced tomatoes

$1/4$ cup honey

$1/4$ cup freshly squeezed lime juice

2 teaspoons salt

$1^{1}/2$ teaspoons freshly ground black pepper

To make the sauce, toast the chiles in a dry skillet over medium-high heat until they are dark and crisp, about 30 seconds on each side. Then soak the chiles in 1 cup of hot water for 10 minutes to soften.

In a saucepan, heat the 2 tablespoons olive oil over medium-high heat. Sauté the garlic and onion until they are tender, but not brown, about 4 minutes. Sprinkle in the cumin and cook 30 seconds more. Stir in the tomatoes, honey, and the softened, drained chiles. Simmer for 15 minutes, until slightly thickened. Add the lime juice, 1 teaspoon salt, and $1/2$ teaspoon pepper. Cool slightly.

(continued)

(continued from page 43)

2 pounds catfish fillets,
or 6 whole, cleaned catfish

1½ cups masa harina

1 teaspoon paprika

½ teaspoon garlic powder

½ teaspoon dried oregano

Vegetable or corn oil for frying

Purée in a food processor or blender, gradually adding the ½ cup olive oil to make a smooth sauce. Set aside or chill until ready to use. Store in an airtight container in the refrigerator for up to 1 month.

To prepare the catfish, mix together the masa harina, 1 teaspoon salt, 1 teaspoon pepper, paprika, garlic powder, and oregano in a shallow dish or pie plate. Dredge the fish fillets in the masa mixture and pat gently to remove the excess breading.

Panfry or deep-fry the catfish in the vegetable oil until it is golden brown, crisp, and just cooked through, about 6 minutes. Drain on paper towels and serve warm with ramekins of warm sauce for dipping.

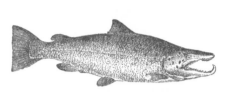

# Alaska's Celebrity Salmon:
# The Copper River King

THE CESSNA 206 lifted off Lake Eyak rising rapidly to the narrow notch in the Heney Mountains, passing through it at approximately 9 P.M., still plenty of light, into the vast Copper River Delta, which opened up before us like a Cecil B. DeMille movie.

Cramped into the plane, and the one behind us, was a mixed bag of seafood paparazzi, including a television news team from Seattle, editors from two seafood magazines, a writer for *Sunset,* a photographer, a chef, and a noted gourmet—all onboard for the arrival of the Copper River king: Alaska's most celebrated salmon.

Most celebrated—and most anticipated. Copper River kings are the first salmon to arrive in Alaskan waters in the spring—first to be captured and first on the market. They arrive after two to four years at sea; fat from feeding on shoals of shrimp, herring, and anchovies; surviving everything from killer whales to high-seas gillnetters, saving the worst for last: the run upriver to their spawning grounds.

About mid-May is when the season opens: whenever a minimum "escapement" passes the electronic fish counters on the river to assure the renewal of the run. Once the numbers are reached, a series of 12- to 24-hour openings commences, sending restaurants and retail markets around the world into a tizzy as they scramble for their share of the booty. The first opening of the season is the wildest because everyone wants to share in the glory of offering the first fish of the season to their customers.

And some want to offer the *very first.* There's a long-standing competition in Seattle (carried to extreme lengths) on who serves (or sells) the first Copper River king of the season—a culinary coup that's guaranteed front-page coverage in the local media.

And this, Wayne Ludvigsen, sitting next to me on the plane, well knew. The managing chef at Ray's Boathouse in Seattle (one of the city's best seafood restaurants), Wayne was the hands-down favorite for this year's winner. As the season had opened only a few hours ago, he appeared to have it in the bag—or so he thought.

*Bump, bump, bump . . .*

The floatplane settled on the silty-green river, into a pandemonium of fishing boats. Gillnets criss-crossed every rip and eddy, the corks bobbing with fish, cash buyers standing at anchor with stacks of $100 bills waiting for the first fish to be delivered. It was a 24-hour opening, the first of the year; projected catch: 28,000 salmon.

We taxied alongside a salmon buyer, the *M/V Tradition,* and climbed aboard. The television crew positioned itself on deck, microphone and camera at the ready, all awaiting the arrival of the celebrity salmon.

Meanwhile, your trusty reporter had stationed himself in the galley next to the coffee urn and a tall stack of $100 bills. Why did I ever give up fishing? The Copper River used to be in my backyard. I taught school in Cordova, the small fishing village from which this "invasion" was launched. I taught during the winter, and what was left of me in the spring went fishing.

*Then I remembered the night a big blow hit the flats, all the boats struggling to stay on anchor, combers crashing on the beach curdling your blood, and young Dave, his first season, anchor line snapping under the strain, drifting through the boats huddled together like scared animals, disappearing into the dark . . . .*

The best salmon maybe, but some of the worst fishing. The reasons are simple enough: a massive spring run-off on the river converging at the delta with huge tides from Prince William Sound. Add the wind, and it's a watery hell. Plus, the delta is so shallow that at low tide some of the boats are left high and dry on sand dunes, lulling you into a false sense of security. Then the tide comes back on little cat's feet, the velocity slowly building until you can hear the silty water grinding against the hull like sandpaper, the river roaring under you like some wild beast. . . .

No, this isn't farmed salmon. When you eat this salmon, you can hear wolves howling in the woods. But why would anyone risk fishing for them? Money, for one thing. A Copper River king fetches up to three times the price of any other salmon, which raises another question: Why so much?

That they are the first salmon of the season is part of it, but only a small part. The main reason is their high fat content. Copper River kings roll into the river as fat as butter balls: rich in omega-3 fatty acid. *Not* the kind of fat we shun, the saturated fat that turns us into heart patients, but fat that slims down our blood—lowers our cholesterol—reducing the incidence of heart disease (as proven in study after study).

But even omega-3, healthful as it is, isn't the reason. It's the taste. One bite and your taste buds are dancing in your mouth: a fish that liquefies on your palate like some rare confection. What makes it so tasty—and so healthful—is the fat.

Other salmon are rich in fat, but few come close to the Copper River king—and the reason is important to understand because it applies to all salmon. The longer the river, the fatter the salmon—and the Copper River is the second longest river in Alaska: a 200-mile gauntlet of gillnets and grizzly bears. Once they enter the river, salmon stop feeding, relying entirely on their reserves of fat to get them to where they're going. The longer the river, the greater the reserves. Copper River kings are genetically programmed to pack a lot of fat to cover the great distance. By contrast, the shorter rivers of western Alaska produce king salmon that look exactly like Copper River kings but are practically tasteless. I know because I used to catch them—and got paid a pittance for my trouble.

The longest river in Alaska, by the way, is the Yukon. True to form, Yukon kings are even fatter and juicier than Copper River kings, but when it gets that good the difference doesn't matter. In any case, the Yukon harvest is much smaller, and almost all of it goes to Japan, where it is processed into salmon flakes used as a flavoring in rice.

At last, the moment had arrived! A gillnetter named *UFO* pulled alongside and started unloading its catch. Big fish, averaging 25 pounds. The television crew sprang into action. . . . A reporter thrust a microphone in front of the fisherman, "What's so special about the Copper River king?" he asked. I knew exactly the answer ("the price, you idiot!").

But he just smiled and kept unloading. Sea lice were still on the salmon, a very good sign. In England, they'd fetch a higher price because the sea lice are evidence that the salmon are fresh from the sea and at their peak. These had just entered the river, the perfect salmon at the perfect time.

The fishing was now getting heavy, boats unloading on every side of us. "These are going to Paris," said the tenderman, setting aside some of the salmon. And to cities around the world—Tokyo, San Francisco, New York . . . and Seattle. The chef from Ray's was beaming. His salmon were already boxed up and on the floatplane. In the morning, they'd be on their way to Seattle. Little did he know that the mayor of Cordova was even now in Seattle parading a Copper River king around town. Everyone called "foul" (she caught it on a fishing rod), but it was all part of the fun.

And it all ends in three to four weeks. The kings that weren't caught (the "escapement") are on their gravel beds, or near them, tattered and torn, mere shadows of what they were when they entered the river.

If you missed the show this year, don't worry. It's been going on for a long time: 10 million years, ever since the end of the Ice Age. But better circle May on your calendar because whatever the price, it's always a sellout performance—and worth every bit of it.

# Perfect Grilled Salmon

Many people don't grill fish at home. They worry that their fish will stick, be raw in the center, or fall through the rack like sawdust if they do something wrong. If this sounds familiar, here are the basic steps to cooking a perfect piece of salmon on the barbecue. When you have mastered the technique, shell out the money for boutique salmon such as Copper River or Yukon River kings. To embellish these fish with anything more than salt, pepper, and perhaps a squeeze of lemon is akin to gilding a lily.

These instructions will help you grill perfect fish.

The day you are cooking, select a firm salmon with slick, shiny skin, no missing scales, and bright eyes. Have the salmon filleted. Make sure the butcher handles it carefully, with two hands, and wraps it flat. If you want him to do all of the work, ask him to leave the skin on, but pull out the pin bones with tweezers. Leaving the skin on the fish is especially good for beginners as it helps to hold the fish together. Skinless fillets have twice the grilling surface. The fish should be cut into fillets of even thickness with long strokes from a sharp knife. A whole salmon fillet is impressive to serve, but nearly impossible to cook evenly because of the varied thickness.

Prepare your grill carefully. It is best to use live coals that are properly preheated. If you must use a gas grill, make sure you use one that can really crank out the BTUs. A grill with a thin, uneven flame and tiny grill surface will not give the best results. Scrub the grill shiny and clean with a steel brush and some oil. Especially dirty grills can be cleaned with oven cleaner. Preheat the grill while you preheat the coals. The grill is ready to use when you can hold your hand about 5 inches from the cooking surface for 2 to 3 seconds.

Don't cook the fish straight out of the fridge. Let the fillets warm at room temperature for as long as it takes to heat the grill or coals, but do not let the fish get warm.

Brush the top of the fish with a very fine layer of oil, then season lightly with salt and pepper. Place the fish fillets skin-side up onto the grill, perpendicular to the grill lines. Close the lid of the grill. Leave a 1-inch-thick fillet of salmon alone for

3 minutes! If the fish is thicker, reduce the heat slightly and leave the fish alone for 4 minutes. The sides of the fish will look cooked and slightly browned. The skin will be dry. Touch the fish with your fingers. The outside edges will feel quite firm and resilient, the center will still be soft and springy. Place a large flat spatula under the far side of the fillet and carefully slip it under the fish. If your grill was clean and you have left it alone, there should be no sticking. If the fish sticks slightly, press the fillet lightly with your free hand and slide the spatula under it. Instead of picking up the fish and flipping it over, simply roll the fillets over. Close the lid and leave the fish alone again, for 3 minutes.

The fish should be perfect. To double check for doneness, press the thickest part of the fillets with your fingers to feel for the springy resilience. Or, break the fish in the center to peer at the thickest interior. A perfectly cooked piece of salmon will not be a uniform pink. The interior of the fish will be slightly darker than the top edges. It will look very moist and just barely break into natural flakes. A sticky, red, raw look means it needs a moment more. Remember that the fish will continue to cook after you lift it from the heat source, so the dark pink interior will be perfect by the time you get everyone to the table.

# Maple-Glazed Salmon Fillets

This is almost as good as dining on a piece of freshly smoked salmon. Marinate the salmon in the sweet glaze for a few hours for moist, flavorful fish. If you want a really quick meal, just brush the sauce onto salmon fillets as they cook. For extra flavor, grill the fish over a hot apple- or alderwood fire.

| Serves 4 |
|---|

**Marinade**

1/2 cup maple syrup

1/4 cup freshly squeezed orange juice

1 teaspoon grated orange zest

Pinch of ground cayenne pepper

4 (6-ounce) boneless, skinless salmon fillets

1/2 teaspoon salt

1/2 teaspoon freshly ground black pepper

To make the marinade, in a shallow, nonreactive dish, mix together the maple syrup, orange juice, orange zest, and cayenne pepper. Place the fish in the marinade, and refrigerate, turning occasionally for up to 24 hours.

Preheat an outdoor grill or a broiler.

Remove the fish from the marinade and let the excess moisture drip off. Season with salt and pepper. Grill or broil the fish for 4 minutes on each side or until the salmon is just barely cooked through. Serve immediately.

# What's in a Name?

 "WHY CAN'T A FISH BE MORE LIKE A CHICKEN?" clucked my friend with indignation. He's a fishmonger, and he was complaining about all the different names for fish—as many as 25 for a single species—that were confusing his customers.

"Not only that, but consider the names: *catfish, dogfish, buffalo, red horse, wolffish, elephant fish*—I'm running a zoo, not a fish market—*suckers, croakers, grunts, groupers*—the names are indecent!—*sheephead, bulbous dreamers, hagfish, porgy, and bass.* . . . How can I sell fish with handles like that?"

"Well, I—"

"Do I offer a special on roach, *Rutilus rutilis* (relative of the carpsucker)—with perhaps a recipe card for poached roach?"

"Gag," I said.

"Gag?" That's another one, *Mycteroperch microlepsis*, common along the South Atlantic coast. They taste like swordfish, but who wants to eat a gag?"

He had a point. Not only are there hundreds of names, but the images many of them conjure up will make you gag. To offset the problem, seafood marketers will sometimes take linguistic liberties, bestowing more glamorous names than the ones the fish were born with: "butterfish" for blackcod, "calamari" for squid, "cape shark" for dogfish, *"loup de mer"* for wolffish, and so on. But this only adds to the problem.

To solve it, our federal fishcrats (the National Marine Fisheries Service) came up with a nomenclature scheme some years ago that classified fish according to their "edibility profile." Thus, catfish, bulbous dreamers, and yellow grunts might all be marketed under the same name (or number) because they taste alike. The scheme made bureaucratic sense, but it didn't work.

Because the names of fish are part of our culture, a reflection of our political history, for example: *emperor fish, kingfish, queenfish, Irish lords, warmouths, slippery dicks* . . . and so on. We don't want to give them up.

A fish's name will often tell a story—for example, mahimahi, a fish you probably know very well because it's so delicious, means "strong strong" in Hawaiian, the exclamation of Hawaiian fishermen years ago when they hooked them on handlines. In Spanish, they're called *dorado,* which means "gold" after the brilliant gold flecks on their sides when they first come out of the water.

"Bullhead!" blurted my friend. (He couldn't stop carping about the names.) "Is there no limit to misnomers?"

There is. A legal limit, anyway. Fish must be sold under a *common name* officially recognized by the Food & Drug Administration. The fish may have more than one common name, but not just any name. (Implicit in the idea of a common name is a wide degree of recognition and acceptance.) Plus, every species has only one Latin name. Hence, king salmon and Chinook salmon are two common names for the same fish, *Oncorhynchus tshawytscha.*

A fish will have more than one common name for various reasons. The more popular a fish, the more common names it will have, varying from region to region. As in the case of *Sciaenops ocellata,* or red drum, known as channel bass in South Carolina and redfish in Louisiana.

Common names evolve out of respect for a species, one that is excellent to eat or catch (or both), but also from more mercenary motives. For example, *Oncorhynchus keta,* widely known in Alaska as dog salmon because Eskimos traditionally fed them to their sled dogs, is more commonly marketed as chum salmon, keta, or silverbrites.

Sometimes a common name evolves with the clear intent of deceiving the consumer by confusing a lower-priced species with a more expensive one, as in the case of *Sebastes ruberrimus,* or yelloweye rockfish, which is allowed in California (but nowhere else) to be sold as red snapper, *Lutjanus campechanus,* an entirely different (and much more expensive) fish. What these two species have in common is red skin, making it easy to confuse them. Of course, folks in California know by now that the "red snapper" they eat in California is not the same as the red snapper they eat in Florida. In fact, it may not be the same in Florida either because two other snappers, the mutton and the silk (also red skinned), are frequently substituted for the real red.

Sometimes fish are named so because of their taste. I once caught a cobia, *Rachycentron canadum,* in the Gulf of Mexico, and my Louisiana guide referred to it as a lemon fish. Why? Because it has a slight (and very delightful) lemony taste.

But many species are left stuck with crappie common names (as in black crappie, *Pomoxis nigromaculatus*). Names like that turn customers off, even though the fish may be quite wonderful to eat (as crappies are).

"We should Hawaiianize the whole system—that's the solution," exclaimed my retailer friend. "Tuna sells better as *ahi.* Dolphin is a snap as *mahimahi* . . . *Opakapaka, opah, ula ula, uku, aku*—these are all names with charisma."

I had to admit he had a point. Hawaiians have a way with naming fish. The longest name of any fish is in Hawaiian, the *humuhumunukunukuapuaa.*

"Now you're talking turkeyfish *(Pterois volitans),*" I said, congratulating him. I recommended he propose the system right away to the FDA (while he was still young). Under his scheme, dogfish would be sold as *bow'au,* crappies as *krapuaas*—and so on. A linguistic renaissance for seafood was in the making.

But for right now, we'll have to live with the old *krapuaa* system of common names. The more you know about them, though, the more fascinating they become. Did you know, for example, that the Dolly Varden, a species of char, is named after a character in a Charles Dickens novel? Miss Varden's pink spotted dress in *Barnaby Rudge* inspired the name. Isn't that interesting?

# Sesame Fried Calamari

Fried squid is a family favorite. Instead of the classic fried calamari rings, I prefer to cut the squid tubes in half and then dredge and fry them. The squid curls into rolls for a lovely presentation and a tender mouthful. For extra flavor and color, sprinkle with hot chile oil, chives, or commercially prepared seaweed sprinkles called *nori furikake*. Make a simple dipping sauce by mixing soy sauce and vinegar.

## Serves 6

1 cup toasted sesame seeds

1/2 cup flour

1 teaspoon salt

1/2 teaspoon freshly ground black pepper

Pinch of ground cayenne pepper

1 pound cleaned calamari tubes

Oil for frying

Hot chile oil for garnish

Snipped chives or seaweed sprinkles for garnish

### Dipping sauce

1/4 cup light soy sauce

1/4 cup rice vinegar or freshly squeezed lemon juice

Make seasoned flour by combining the sesame seeds, flour, salt, black pepper, and cayenne in a food processor or blender. Pulse into a fine flour, but do not overmix or the sesame seeds will become pastelike. Pour the flour into a shallow dish and set aside.

Slit the calamari tubes in half lengthwise.

Dredge 3 or 4 calamari fillets in the sesame-seasoned flour and panfry them in oil over medium to medium-high heat. Cook only until they have curled and are golden brown, about 30 to 45 seconds on each side. Remove the calamari from the pan, pat dry with paper towels, and continue with remaining calamari.

To make the dipping sauce, combine the ingredients in a small bowl.

Garnish the calamari with drops of hot chile oil and a light sprinkling of chives or seaweed sprinkles. Serve with the dipping sauce alongside.

# Microwaved Moi

Seafood alternatives: Pomfret; Rex Sole; Any Small Whole Fish or Tender Fish Fillet

*Moi* (rhymes with *boy*) is the Hawaiian name for the Pacific threadfin, a fish once reserved exclusively for native kings. My first taste came in the grimy breakroom of a Hawaiian seafood wholesaler. It was simply seasoned and served on a styrofoam tray straight from the microwave. The small fish was perfectly cooked, with gently flaking, bright white flesh and a marvelously clean, sweet flavor. Wherever you live, there surely is a local specialty fish that can be simply seasoned with these island flavors and zapped for a few minutes with equally delicious results. *Moi* is now being successfully farmed and can occasionally be found during Hawaiian seafood promotions and at top restaurants on the mainland.

### Serves 1

1 moi (or any 8 to 10-ounce whole fish or tender fish fillet)

1 teaspoon sesame oil

1/8 teaspoon Hawaiian red salt (or substitute kosher or sea salt)

Pinch of crushed red chile flakes

2 green onions, green parts only, sliced

Place the fish on a microwave-safe plate. Sprinkle evenly with all of the ingredients. Cover with plastic wrap and microwave for 3 minutes on high. Let rest for 2 minutes and serve.

*Note:* Fish is great in the microwave, but if you prefer, follow the same instructions but place the platter in the basket of a bamboo steamer and cook over simmering water for 8–10 minutes or until the fish is opaque throughout.

# Dining Out

MORE THAN HALF of the seafood consumed in America is eaten in restaurants—that's a fact. What I want to know is how all these people can afford it? I know I can't, but I do it anyway. Restaurants are one of life's great pleasures, and seafood restaurants are especially wonderful because they give us a chance to expand our seafood knowledge. With hundreds of fish and shellfish species to learn about, we need all the help we can get.

And what a pleasant way to do it. But a good seafood restaurant is hard to find. This is because good seafood, to say nothing of *great* seafood, requires commitment; it never happens accidentally, and not every restaurant is willing to pay the price. The ones that do are to be treasured; the ones that don't are to be avoided—and it's up to us to know the difference.

Here are some tips that will help you identify a seafood restaurant with commitment:

*Always judge a seafood restaurant by its cover.* By its menu, that is. One glance is all it takes. The salmon is "scrumptious!" but does it say what kind of salmon it is? (There are six species, each distinctly different.)

The crab cakes sound good, but if the crab is incognito, reconsider. If it's Dungeness crab, on the other hand, you know it's good.

The lobster tail ("drenched in butter") is from where? No one knows, except "it comes in plastic bags." There's a huge difference between, say, coldwater tails from

Australia and warmwater tails from Brazil, the former tastier and more tender (and at a much higher cost).

A seafood restaurant with commitment is proud of what it serves—and will tell you in detail on the menu: Nova Scotia sea scallops, Monterey Bay squid, Idaho rainbow trout, Alaska red king crab, Prince Edward Island rope-cultured mussels . . .

*Never ask the server if the fish is "fresh."* The answer is always the same: "Of course!" ("It just came in the door." "The boat's tied up outside." And so on.) I've never known a restaurant yet that didn't serve "fresh" fish, which means anything from wriggling to rotten. *Fresh* is the trickiest word in seafood because to people in the trade it has no reference to quality, only to the fact that it wasn't frozen. Ask more intelligent questions such as:

"What's in season?"

"What's your best local fish?"

"What does your chef recommend tonight?"

If the server has to go back to the kitchen to find out, that's fine. Let them know you're there. If the recommendation that comes out of the kitchen is the highest priced item on the menu, you might be in the wrong restaurant.

*Never order "sea bass" in a restaurant unless you know what kind of sea bass it is.* Chilean sea bass, black sea bass, California sea bass . . . are all acceptable, but "sea bass" without a prefix can mean: "We don't know what kind of fish this is, so we called it sea bass. . . ." or "That's what they told us to say. . . ." or "It's really shark, but we don't want you to know. . . ."

Of course, the chances are it's Chilean sea bass (Patagonian toothfish), an excellent fish very properly called sea bass.

Missing prefixes can be a problem, but also added prefixes that are vague and misleading: such as *ocean* sea bass or *deep-sea* sea bass, which could be anything.

*Never order a fish advertised as "fresh" when it's out of season,* because something is "fishy." Probably it has been frozen and thawed (it's really "fresh thawed"), or poached (and I don't mean the cooking method), or it's not the fish you think it is (or they think it is). In any case, this is not a seafood restaurant with commitment. ("Sorry, we really meant fresh-frozen.")

*Don't hesitate to test your waiter's seafood knowledge.* This will tell you how committed the restaurant is to good service, which is very important when it comes to the intricacies of seafood. For example, you could order your oysters by their Latin names. Admittedly, this would be going too far, but I know seafood restaurants where this wouldn't ruffle the waiters one bit—because the restaurant has made it a point to teach them.

*Do they know their oysters?* The final test of a good seafood restaurant is the quality of its oyster service. To know this is to know the restaurant. Whether you like oysters or not is beside the point. There are three criteria: *variety, quality,* and *presentation.*

*Variety* is self-explanatory. Oysters vary from region to region much as wines do. (What would life be with only one wine or one oyster to choose from?) Several varieties should be offered.

*Quality* refers to freshness. Unlike wines, oysters don't get better with age. No more than seven days from the water, please. If you're having oysters on the half-shell, they should be opened just before serving—or at least that day.

*Presentation* means how the oysters look on the plate: no broken shell in the meat, the adductor muscles completely severed so that each oyster is free-floating in its own liquor ready to be slurped down.

There are other tips I could give you about eating in restaurants . . . *never order whole lobster if you're wearing a new Givenchy tie*—unless you're wearing a bib, in which case, *never sit next to someone wearing a new Givenchy tie. . . .* But the main thing is to find a restaurant that shares your passion for seafood—then bring what you learn back to your own kitchen, where the best seafood is always served.

And one other thing. If anyone asks why you're eating out so much, just say you're "doing research."

# Roasted Trout Stuffed with Spinach, Hazelnuts, and Blue Cheese

Roasting whole fish in high heat crisps up the outside while keeping the flesh inside moist and juicy. Have your fishmonger butterfly the fish for an elegant, boneless presentation.

| Serves 4 |
|---|

1 tablespoon butter or margarine

1 cup chopped onion

1 teaspoon minced garlic

1 bunch fresh spinach, blanched and squeezed dry, or 1 (10-ounce) box frozen spinach, squeezed of excess moisture

1/2 cup toasted hazelnuts, coarsely chopped

2 ounces crumbled blue cheese

1 tablespoon unseasoned bread crumbs

Pinch of freshly grated nutmeg

Salt

Freshly ground black pepper

4 whole trout, about 3/4 pound each, cleaned

1 tablespoon olive oil

Preheat the oven to 500°.

Arrange a lightly oiled rack in the bottom of a roasting pan.

Melt the butter in a small skillet over medium heat. Add the onion and garlic, and sauté until soft and aromatic, about 3 minutes. Let cool.

In a medium bowl, mix together the onion and garlic mixture, spinach, hazelnuts, blue cheese, and bread crumbs. Season with nutmeg, salt, and pepper.

Stuff each trout with one-fourth of the spinach mixture. The fish should be plump without bursting with filling. Brush the outside of the fish lightly with olive oil, sprinkle with additional salt and pepper, and place on the prepared rack.

Roast the trout in the oven. Cook until the fish no longer springs back when gently poked at the thickest part, about 15 minutes. Carefully lift the fish from the pan. Serve immediately.

# Grilled Columbia River Sturgeon with Sweet Corn and Jerusalem Artichokes

Seafood alternatives: Scallops, Halibut, Red Snapper, Salmon

When sturgeon fillets are resting next to bright white halibut or sea bass, it is tempting to pass by the mottled and blotchy prehistoric fish. Please don't. Select fish with bright yellow streaks of fat and moist, clear flesh and you won't regret it. Jerusalem artichokes are sometimes sold as "sunchokes." They have the flavor of an artichoke and the texture of a waxy potato.

### Serves 4

4 (6 to 8-ounce) sturgeon steaks or fillets

**Marinade**

¹/₂ cup olive oil

¹/₄ cup aged sherry vinegar (or good red wine vinegar)

1 shallot, peeled and chopped

4 to 6 cloves garlic, chopped

4 sprigs oregano, bruised and torn

4 tablespoons unsalted butter

1 cup peeled, diced Jerusalem artichokes (about ¹/₂ pound)

4 cloves garlic, chopped

¹/₄ pound ham, chopped

Marinate the sturgeon in the olive oil, vinegar, shallot, garlic, and oregano overnight, turning occasionally.

Preheat an outdoor grill or broiler.

Lift the sturgeon from the marinade and let the excess oil drip off. Grill the sturgeon for 5 minutes on each side. It is difficult to overcook sturgeon, but the fish can be quite tough when undercooked. Pierce the fish with a knife in the center to double check for doneness. The center should look white and opaque through and be quite tender. Remove the fish to a serving platter and keep it warm while you are preparing the sauce.

(continued)

(continued from page 61)

1 cup sweet corn cut from the cob (2 ears of corn)

$1/4$ cup medium sherry or dry white wine

$3/4$ cup chicken stock

$1/2$ teaspoon salt

$1/2$ teaspoon freshly ground black pepper

1 tablespoon chopped fresh parsley

1 teaspoon chopped fresh oregano, or $1/4$ teaspoon dried

1 teaspoon chopped fresh sage, or $1/4$ teaspoon dried

1 cup diced tomatoes

2 shallots, peeled and thinly sliced

1 tablespoon flour

Vegetable oil for frying

Melt half of the butter in a large skillet over medium heat. Add the Jerusalem artichokes and garlic and sauté until the artichokes are golden brown, 5 minutes. Add the ham and cook 4 minutes more, until the ham has browned. Add the corn and stir to mix. Deglaze with the sherry and add the stock. Bring the sauce to a boil, season with salt, pepper, parsley, oregano, and sage. Simmer for 3 to 4 minutes to reduce slightly. Stir in the remaining butter and the tomatoes.

Toss the shallots in the flour and fry in $1/2$ inch of vegetable oil in a small pan until they are golden brown and crisp, about $1^1/2$ minutes. Remove and drain on crumpled paper towels.

Spoon a generous amount of the vegetable sauce over the sturgeon and garnish with the fried shallots. Serve immediately.

# Orrechiette with Alaska King Crab and Chard

Seafood alternatives: Sea bass, Scallops, Dungeness Crab, Lobster

Orrechiette is a traditional pasta shaped like little ears; the tiny pasta cups maintain a firm texture while capturing the flavorful sauce. King crab is almost always sold as frozen, precooked legs. The sweet crab should be only warmed through for best flavor and texture. This is an excellent way to make a little bit of this very pricey crab go a long way.

### Serves 4 to 6

2 tablespoons olive oil

1/2 cup diced onion

4 cloves garlic, thickly sliced

1/4 teaspoon crushed red pepper flakes

1/2 cup dry white wine

1 cup chicken stock or clam nectar

1 bunch chard, tough stems removed, chopped (about 8 cups loosely packed)

1 pound dry orrechiette pasta

1/2 teaspoon salt

1/2 teaspoon freshly ground black pepper

Bring a large pot of salted water to a boil.

Heat 2 tablespoons of the olive oil in a large skillet over medium heat. Add the onion, garlic, and red pepper flakes, and cook until the onion is soft, but not brown, about 4 minutes. Add the white wine and stock. Increase the heat to medium high and simmer to reduce by half, 4 to 5 minutes. Add the chard and cook 2 minutes more, until the chard is wilted and tender. Set aside.

(continued)

(continued from page 63)

**1 teaspoon finely grated lemon zest**

**4 tablespoons extra virgin olive oil**

**3/4 pound king crab, shells removed, cut into bite-sized chunks**

Meanwhile cook the pasta according to the manufacturer's directions. Drain well and return the pasta to the empty pot. Pour the chard mixture over the pasta and add the salt, pepper, lemon zest, extra virgin olive oil, and crab. Cook the pasta and sauce over medium heat until the pasta has absorbed some of the sauce, 1 to 2 minutes. Pour into a warm serving dish. Serve immediately.

# The Bear Truth About Salmon

I'VE HEARD IT SAID THAT A BEAR can smell salmon through a can. I don't know about that, but I know they can smell it through the water because I saw one do it. And lucky for me, too. I was fishing on the Big River in the Katmai National Park in southwest Alaska (having flown in from the native village of Iliamna), when I noticed two brown bears, a sow and a cub, watching me wistfully from the opposite bank. Most people think bears all look alike—and vice versa—but not true. The two bears watching me had striking red hair and a hungry look that reminded me of some of my Irish relatives.

Anyway, I continued fishing with one eye on the river and one on the bears. Meanwhile, the rest of my group had gathered around the floatplane, which was beached farther downstream, getting ready to board for the flight back to the lodge. The pilot, a grizzled veteran of these parts, had both eyes on the bears.

He should have had one of them on the guide, a young fellow from Vermont who was in the act of committing a seafood atrocity. He was filleting several salmon I had caught earlier and rinsing them in the river—a seafood faux pas that nearly cost us our lives.

*Never fillet a fish before its time, especially when a grizzly bear is watching.*

Suddenly, mama bear and baby bear were swimming toward the plane—no doubt in a state of olfactory ecstasy over the smell of freshly cut salmon.

Seeing the danger, the guide frantically started packing the salmon into the pontoon of the plane, raising a very interesting question: If a bear can smell a salmon through a can, can he (or she, in this case) smell it through the pontoon of a plane? And what would the bear do if it did?

The answers to these questions must have occurred to the pilot at the same time they did me. In fact, we had heard a report earlier in the week of some fishermen going back to their plane only to find it shredded by bears looking for the salmon stored inside. "Popped 'er open like a Budweiser can . . ."

We both freaked.

"My plane!"

"My salmon!"

The guide, on strict orders from the pilot, was now tossing my fillets into the river as a peace offering to the bears. *Damn!* The engine cranked over, as I huffed it for the plane, the faces of the passengers—we had a group of naturalists aboard from San Francisco—pressed against the windows, their eyes riveted on the bears that were now in the shallows galloping toward the plane.

Then I heard a horrible growling close behind me. "My God, I've eaten my last fish. . . ."

But the bears had stopped short of the plane and were in a tug-of-war over one of the carcasses the guide had discarded in the river (which I was going to use for smoking!).

I clambered into the plane and, in seconds, we were in the air—barely escaping.

Is there a lesson in this? Of course. Poor seafood handling. The sooner a fish is filleted, the sooner it will spoil. Always have your fish dealer cut your fillets fresh from a whole fish—or, even better, do it at home just before cooking. Think of it in terms of your own flesh: Never bare more than the occasion demands.

And never rinse a fillet unless you dropped it on the floor—or have reason to doubt its cleanliness. Rinsing washes away vitamins and dampens the flavor—not to mention other problems if you happen to be in bear country.

This reminds me of another bear story. A sport fisherman in Petersburg, Alaska, was cleaning a salmon on the dock, when he felt what he thought was his partner's hot breath on the back of his neck. After saying a few words and getting no answer, he turned around to see a bear admiring his work.

Alaska grizzlies are great connoisseurs of salmon and, were they able, could write a book on salmon quality. They eat only fresh salmon, eschewing the carcasses rotting on the bank in favor of live salmon, which they are very adept at catching. And they know their salmon species as well as anyone, preferring king salmon over pinks or silvers because kings are fatter and juicier—and will serve them better during their winter hibernation. If the fishing is really good, they'll eat only the bellies, leaving the rest to rot. The bellies are the best part of the salmon (as any native Alaskan knows) because they have the most fat; plus there's the added bonus of salmon caviar.

Another thing about Alaskan grizzlies is that they know the fattest salmon are those that come in fresh from the sea. Thus, you see them congregating in the deltas and river mouths, no doubt partly because they can't wait for their salmon dinner, but also because they know these are the quality fish.

Black bears aren't that big on salmon, preferring the higher elevations where they browse on berries—as far away from grizzlies as possible. Grizzlies are bad. On the flight between Iliamna and Big River, I noted to the pilot that I had never seen so many bull moose in my life, but not one cow or calf. He just smiled at my naivete. "You don't see any black bears down there either, do you?"

No, but I did count more than 30 grizzlies. How to tell the difference between the two? I once asked a game warden that question. "If a bear is chasing you and you climb up a tree and it climbs up after you, you know it's a black bear."

Good luck.

# Breakfast Fry Up

Seafood alternatives: Any Freshly Caught Fish

This is possibly the best meal in the universe. Nothing beats freshly caught fish for breakfast, especially when it is fried with potatoes, onions, and bacon. To finish it up, add a couple of eggs, some toast, and plenty of hot, black coffee.

### Serves 2

6 slices bacon, cut into 1/2-inch pieces

1 onion, sliced

1 medium potato, peeled and diced

2 tablespoons flour

1/2 teaspoon salt

1/2 teaspoon freshly ground black pepper

Pinch of ground cayenne pepper

2 (4-ounce) boneless salmon fillets or any small lake fish

4 eggs

Fry the bacon and onion on a large griddle or skillet until lightly colored and tender, about 6 minutes. Drain off half of the fat and reserve. (If your bacon is especially lean, you may need to add additional butter or vegetable oil.) Fry the potato pieces with the bacon and onion until they are tender on the inside and crispy on the outside, 12 to 13 minutes, stirring and flipping occasionally. Remove the vegetables to a warm platter and set aside. Reheat the pan with the reserved bacon fat.

Mix together the flour, salt, black pepper, and cayenne on a large plate. Dredge the fish in the seasoned flour and pat lightly to shake off the excess. Fry the fish over medium heat until the outside is golden brown and crispy, about 4 minutes. Flip and fry on the other side until just opaque through the thickest part, about 3 to 4 minutes longer.

If desired, cook the eggs to your preference and serve hot with the fish, crispy potatoes, toast, and coffee.

# Salmon Steaks with Sweet Onions and Apples

Seafood alternatives: Trout, Arctic Char, Bluefish

Whole dinners wrapped in foil and cooked in the coals of a campfire or on an outdoor grill make a carefree summer meal. Any combination of seafood and vegetables can be used, but try to pick items that will cook evenly. Here, slices of tart apples, sweet onions, and salmon steaks are cooked together with a touch of butter and lemon. The best apples for this dish are Fuji, Gala, or Gravenstein.

**Serves 4**

2 tablespoons butter or margarine

1 sweet onion (such as Walla Walla), sliced

2 medium apples, peeled, cored, and sliced

4 (8 to 10-ounce) salmon steaks

1 lemon, sliced

1/2 teaspoon salt

1/2 teaspoon freshly ground black pepper

Cut 4 large pieces of heavy-duty aluminum foil about 14 inches square. Rub the center of each square with a little of the butter. Evenly distribute the onion and apple slices on the pieces of foil. Top with the salmon steaks, lemon slices, and the remaining butter. Season with salt and pepper.

Wrap each packet securely, tightly sealing the seams. Nestle the packets in low coals for about 20 minutes. To check, carefully remove one packet from the heat and open to see if the salmon is cooked through. Serve immediately.

If a campfire is not in the plans anytime soon, cook the salmon packets on a preheated barbecue grill or in a 400° oven until the packet juices are sizzling and the fish is opaque through, 12 to 15 minutes.

# The Nose Knows

 "WHAT'S IT SMELL LIKE?"

"Excuse me?"

"Fish—what's it supposed to smell like?"

I was standing at the fish counter trying to get the fishmonger to cut some fresh salmon steaks (fresh-cut is always better) when a fellow consumer accosted me.

"Well, that's simple enough," I said. "A fish smells like a fish—what else would it smell like?"

"But . . ."

"If it doesn't smell like a fish, don't eat it," I advised. "In fact, throw it away!"

The fishmonger was now giving me the evil eye. There went my custom cut.

"On the other hand," I felt compelled to continue, "it shouldn't smell *too much* like a fish. If it smells too much like a fish, don't buy it, either."

"You mean, if it smells . . . *fishy.*"

Shhhhhhhh!

An alarm went off in the fishmonger. He spun around like a bass on a school of minnows. "Who said that?"

"Not us, honest!"

"Fishy" is the 'F' word of seafood: the smell of decomposition. Good seafood never smells fishy—and will never make your kitchen stink. In fact, you can hardly smell

**70**

it at all. The smell is strongest when you first unwrap it from the grocery store, a quick whiff of the seashore, but it quickly dissipates if it's really fresh. The smell of spoiled (fishy) fish, on the other hand, lingers on—and on.

The smell of fish is unique, instantly recognizable—but very difficult to describe. Even the FDA, which sniffs tons of it every year (to ensure its wholesomeness), can't describe its smell. Either it smells good or it doesn't. If it doesn't, it's confiscated.

"The nose knows," says Debra DeVlieger, an FDA fish inspector whose proboscis is an agency treasure. DeVlieger flies all over Alaska sniffing seafood, but she says she has no secrets. Like the writer Gertrude Stein, who declared, "A rose is a rose is a rose," DeVlieger will say only, "A salmon is a salmon is a salmon."

In the end, all you can do is smell enough seafood to know when it's good or not good. In other words (as with wine), training is essential. So when you buy fish, be sure to give it a good sniff. Once you've smelled good seafood—and bad (and all the degrees in between)—you'll never forget it. Though smells are hard to describe, the memory of them stays with us far longer than words.

"The quickest way to stimulate memory is through smell. The memory of smell is far greater than the memory of words—the fastest way to affect emotion. Smell goes directly to the cortex," explains Dr. Alan Hirsch, a neurologist at the Smell & Taste Research Foundation in Chicago.

According to the *Encyclopedia Britannica,* smell is "10,000 times more powerful than taste." Taste is largely an illusion, anyway. What you smell is what you taste. (The proof is simple enough. Hold your nose and you can't taste a thing, not even an onion.) "Almost all taste is really smell," says Dr. Hirsch. "The odors of what we put in our mouths pass through our nasal cavity as we eat . . ."

Some people are gifted sniffers. DeVlieger is one of them. She has some great stories about sniffing seafood, some of them downright scary. Imagine a small woman going into a fish plant somewhere in the wilds of western Alaska armed with nothing more than an FDA baseball cap and a badge. There are maybe a hundred people working on the floor, the place awash in salmon being unloaded from salmon tenders stacked up at the dock. She makes her rounds testing the fish with her nose, then tells the foreman, who barely has the time to listen to her, to stop production, everything in the plant is being confiscated. Thousands upon thousands of dollars worth of fish.

"Why?" he asks, unbelieving.

"Because the bacteria level is too high."

"How do you know?"

"I can smell it."

"It smells okay to me," he says, looming over her, his face furious.

And so on. But the FDA laboratory always bears out her findings.

Of course, there are other organoleptic methods for testing seafood quality—*organoleptic* being the fancy word the FDA uses for testing fish by using the senses. Your eyes, for example. Look at the color of the gills. Are they a healthy looking red or a dark brown? (Some importers require the gills be left in the fish so they can see the quality, an important indicator.) Are the eyes shiny and bright—or sunken and dull? Are most of the scales intact? Are there any signs of bruising or rough handling? If you have only the flesh to look at, does it have a nice, shiny luster or is it dull and grayish looking? And touch. Is the flesh of the fish resilient? Does it spring back when you touch it or is a dent left in the flesh?

All of these are important, but none more so than the sense of smell. So smell more fish, you'll enjoy it, and you'll become a seafood expert. Start by seeing how long it takes to smell the seafood department in your grocery store after you walk in. If you can smell it before you get to it, tell the fishmonger you're confiscating his fish. Better have a hat and badge, though. If there are any questions, just say, "The nose knows."

And remembers. The good smells are the best part. A whiff of steamed clams and I'm suddenly in a kitchen in Newport, Rhode Island, circa 1948, my mother standing over a steaming pot, the memory slowly taking shape in my nostrils. . . .

The nose knows, the nose remembers.

# Potato Salad Niçoise

Salade niçoise is a classic French dish that is traditionally served as a composed salad. This is a variation on the theme, perfect for summertime dinners or a potluck party. If you have a piece of tuna that is not sashimi grade, this is an excellent way to serve it.

| Serves 6 |
|---|

2 pounds small red potatoes

$1/4$ cup red wine vinegar

$1/2$ pound green beans, stemmed

1 bunch kale, tough stems removed, chopped

10 to 12 ounces fresh tuna

1 cup thinly sliced red onion

$1/2$ cup niçoise or other cured black olives

$1/2$ cup olive oil

2 tablespoons chopped fresh parsley

If you have sashimi-grade tuna, sear the outside briefly and serve the tuna in slices. However, this dish is also excellent with tuna that is not sashimi grade. Simply grill, broil, or poach the tuna until it is cooked through. Cool, and then flake with a fork.

Simmer the potatoes in salted water until tender. Remove from the heat, drain. When the potatoes are cool enough to handle, cut them into bite-sized pieces and gently toss with half of the vinegar. Set aside.

(continued)

(continued from page 73)

1 teaspoon chopped fresh thyme

$^1/_2$ teaspoon chopped fresh rosemary

2 cloves garlic, minced or pressed

1 teaspoon Dijon mustard

1 teaspoon anchovy paste (optional)

$^1/_2$ teaspoon salt

$^1/_2$ teaspoon freshly ground black pepper

2 tomatoes, cut into wedges, for garnish

2 hard-boiled eggs, cut into wedges, for garnish

Separately blanch the green beans and kale in boiling, salted water and rinse with cold water to stop the cooking and drain well. Toss the potatoes with the green beans, kale, tuna, onion, and olives.

In a small bowl, whisk together the olive oil, remaining vinegar, parsley, thyme, rosemary, garlic, mustard, anchovy paste, salt, and pepper. Toss the salad with the dressing. Pour onto a serving dish and garnish with tomato wedges and hard-boiled eggs.

# Macadamia-Crusted Tilapia with Orange-Chile Sweet and Sour Sauce

Seafood alternatives: Mahimahi, Hawaiian Snapper, Halibut

Tilapia are everywhere these days. They are easily farmed and therefore cheap and readily available. Whole tilapia are often sold out of live tanks by fishmongers. It is also common to find fillets in better seafood counters or in the freezer shelves. Tilapia is a simple, mild, slightly watery whitefish, so a flavorful preparation such as this is recommended.

## Serves 4

1/2 cup orange juice

1/2 cup very finely chopped or ground macadamia nuts

3 tablespoons flour

1/2 teaspoon salt plus more to taste

1/4 teaspoon freshly ground black pepper plus more to taste

4 (4 to 5-ounce) skinless tilapia fillets

2 to 3 tablespoons peanut oil or vegetable oil

1/4 cup chopped onion

1/2 cup chopped green bell pepper, seeded

1 clove garlic, minced

Pour the orange juice into a shallow dish or plate. In another shallow dish or plate, combine the macadamia nuts and flour with 1/2 teaspoon salt and 1/4 teaspoon pepper. Dip the tilapia fillets in the orange juice, and then dredge each fillet into the nut mixture. Carefully brush or shake off any excess breading. Reserve the juice to prepare the sauce.

Fry the fillets in half of the oil in a large, nonstick skillet over medium-high heat. Cook the tilapia about 2 to 3 minutes on each side, or until the nuts are golden brown and the fish is just opaque through. Remove fillets to a platter and keep them warm while preparing the sauce.

(continued)

(continued from page 75)

1 small hot red chile, seeded and finely chopped, or ¼ teaspoon dried red chile flakes

1 tablespoon grated orange zest

2 tablespoons cider vinegar

2 tablespoons brown sugar

1 teaspoon cornstarch

2 tablespoons water

Wipe out the pan and swirl in the remaining oil. Decrease the heat to medium and sauté the onion, bell pepper, and garlic until soft and aromatic, about 3 minutes. Add the chile and orange zest and stir in the vinegar, brown sugar, and the reserved orange juice. Stir the cornstarch into the water and mix well. Add to the sauce. Simmer until the sauce thickens slightly and is shiny. Season with salt and pepper to taste. Pour sauce over fish fillets and serve immediately.

# Brazilian Shrimp Fritters

Seafood alternatives: Rock Shrimp, White Fish

There is a photograph in the old Time/Life International series cookbooks of a large Brazilian woman in a tropical marketplace, sitting on a stool frying crispy shrimp fritters. This photo always tempts me. Although these fritters may not be authentic, they are inspired by the flavors of Brazil and make a great party food or spicy appetizer.

**Serves 4 to 6
(makes 22 fritters)**

4 cups peeled and grated sweet potatoes

1/2 pound shrimp meat, chopped

1 cup grated onion

2 cloves garlic, minced

1 red chile pepper, seeded and minced

1/3 cup flour

1/2 cup coconut milk

2 eggs

1/2 teaspoon salt

1/2 teaspoon freshly ground black pepper

Vegetable oil or peanut oil for deep-frying

In a large bowl, combine the sweet potato, shrimp, onion, garlic, chile pepper, flour, coconut milk, eggs, salt, and pepper, and mix to form a thick batter.

(continued)

(continued from page 77)

### Dip

1/2 cup rice vinegar or white wine vinegar

2 tablespoons Sambal Oeleck or other hot pepper sauce

Heat 3 or 4 inches of oil in a deep fryer, heavy pan, or wok to 360°. Form the batter into balls about 1 1/2 to 2 inches. Carefully spoon 3 or 4 fritters into the hot oil, being careful not to overcrowd the pan. Cook the fritters for 2 minutes, turning once, until they are golden brown and cooked through. Lift out of the oil and place them on a rack covered with crumpled paper towels to drain. Sprinkle the fritters with a little extra salt. To prepare the dip, mix the vinegar and hot pepper sauce in a small bowl. Serve immediately.

# The Great White:
# A Seafood Adventure

"WHAT COULD I DO?" exclaimed Alberto Ellena, president of the seafood company Pesquera Grimar, gesticulating over his *ensalada de mero*. He was recalling his early days exporting Chilean sea bass to the United States. "My loyalty went to the United States, but the sea bass went to Japan."

We were having lunch at Ellena's favorite restaurant in Santiago, a posh Italian bistro called Grissini on *Avenida Bosque*. Aldo Guida, the chef, was preparing *mero*—sea bass—in different styles to demonstrate its amazing versatility.

"You should export this fish only to the United States," I said to Ellena, savoring the sumptuous *mero*, which melted in my mouth like butter. If you haven't tasted this fish yourself, the best is yet to come.

Between courses, Ellena told me the history of this remarkable fish. It was "discovered" off Chile by deepwater trawlers, mostly foreign vessels fishing under the auspices of General Pinochet. How it escaped notice of Chile's mainly artisanal fleet is understandable considering the incredible depths the sea bass inhabits: down to 5,000 feet. Which explains why it is sometimes called *bacalao de profundidad*— "cod of the deep."

But sea bass is no cod; nor is it, for that matter, a sea bass, but a toothfish—technically a Patagonian toothfish, *Dissostichus eleginoides.* The species to which it is most similar from a culinary point of view (but not biologically) is the sablefish *(Anoplopoma fimbria),* another loner of the deep. Both species are favorite winter fish of the Japanese because of their high fat content, a comfort in colder weather.

Ahhh! *Rapsodia di Tortelli con Mero e Scampi* (Sea Bass Ravioli with Shrimp Sauce)! *Mucho gusto!*

Ellena ordered another bottle of Chilean cabernet—red wine for *real* whitefish—and we dove into the ravioli with wonder.

"Aldo, this is genius!" I exclaimed. Aldo was standing at the table, unshaven, wearing a gold earring and a baseball cap. "No, it's Italian," he said.

The saga of the sea bass (the accepted common name in the United States) is legendary in the seafood trade. California was where it all started in the mid-1980s, when Ellena was living in Redondo Beach, barely able to speak English. He had to do something so he started importing "Chilean sea bass" from his homeland.

"The demand was unbelievable," he recalled, "and everyone wanted the fish *fresh* . . . and there was only one flight a day from Santiago to Miami—not like today, when there are as many as seven."

So the pipeline was jammed most of the time, and the quality was not always perfect. Sometimes the shipments were bumped in favor of fruit and left waiting on the tarmac for the next flight, the ice melting in the sweltering sun. But problems aside, Chilean sea bass was catching on—not only in California but across the country.

Then, the eye of the Japanese fell on the fairest of fish, the marvelous *mero.* Their economy booming, they had the yen to control the market, plus they were already in Chile investing heavily in the farmed salmon industry, which was just getting started. Salmon in South America? Seems strange, but Chile has always been a country of paradox—the oldest democracy in South America and yet (at the time) under a brutal dictatorship: a country of salmon and swordfish, parrots and penguins, apples and papayas . . .

Anyway, the Japanese saw, they tasted, they conquered the market.

California—and, by now, major cities across the country—were bereft of their newly discovered sea bass. To those who knew the fish, it was no small deprivation. Its whiter-than-white flesh, melt-in-your mouth texture, buttery taste—clearly this was a fish without parallel. The demand was terrific, but the Japanese bubble had yet to burst, and the Wonder of Whitefish went East.

Then, in the early 1990s, Argentina discovered the species off its coast, quickly fishing it down to the brink. The same story in Chile. The hunt was on for new grounds. Pockets of toothfish were discovered off the Falkland Islands—and on across the South Atlantic to Prince Edward Island off South Africa. Australia found a resource hidden away in the depths off Heard Island . . . and so it went. Fleets of vessels flying flags from more than a dozen nations were relentlessly hunting the species across the subpolar regions of the world, freezing it at sea and selling it for stunning prices.

All the worst for the Patagonian toothfish. An international quota system was introduced, but how do you enforce a fishery that takes place near the Antarctic Circle? Piracy was rampant. A biological horror story was in the making.

Then the tide began to turn—slightly. Argentina and Chile introduced tough quota systems. Enforcement was beefed up. A certification system was introduced in international waters stemming the flow of illegal fish into the market. Some major busts were made at sea. The Patagonian toothfish was slowly crawling back to sustainability—or so everyone hoped.

And the quality has never been better. Most of the sea bass you see in the market today has been frozen at sea—as opposed to being on ice for weeks on end. Even Ellena, who pioneered the "fresh" market in the United States, agrees the frozen-at-sea product is a vast improvement over the "fresh" fish of the early days. Not to say fresh isn't available—and better than ever—most of it still coming from Chile. Plus, the Japanese bubble went pop, making sea bass more available to U.S. consumers. The bad part is the price—$13.99 a pound last time I looked.

Why is this fish worth so much money? What makes the toothfish so toothsome? The Antarctic explains some of it. No flimsy-fleshed fish this. Packed with "antifreeze"—fat—and firm of flesh to handle the depths, the sea bass has the best of both worlds: sturdy on one hand, melts in your mouth on the other. And the flesh is a stunning white. For this reason, you will always know it in the market—that and the price.

Ah, *mejillas!* Aldo had outdone himself! I speak—rather I *sing*—of sea bass cheeks!

*"Mucho gusto, senor!"* and I toasted the chef and my friend Alberto, who was one of the first to bring us this fish, and to the sea bass itself, Wonder of Whitefish, that it may ever survive—and thrive—in the freezing depths of the austral seas.

# Ginger-Miso Marinated Sea Bass

Seafood alternatives: Salmon, Black Cod, Tuna, Bluefish

This marinade is absolutely perfect with rich fish. Miso is a fermented soybean paste that is often available in the refrigerator section of better grocery stores. The lighter the color the milder the flavor. Here the fish is broiled, but it is also fabulous when prepared on an outdoor grill.

**Serves 4**

**Marinade**

1/4 cup miso

1/4 cup sugar

1/4 cup sake or dry white wine

1 tablespoon grated or minced peeled, fresh ginger

4 (6-ounce) Chilean sea bass fillets or steaks

2 green onions, sliced, for garnish

To make the marinad, stir together the miso, sugar, sake, and ginger. Spread the thick marinade generously on all sides of the fish and let rest in the refrigerator for at least 1 hour.

Preheat a broiler. Place the broiler rack so the fish will be about 6 inches away from the heat source.

Leave the marinade on the fish and then cook the fish on one side only until it is opaque throughout and easily flakes, 8 to 9 minutes for a 3/4-inch-thick fillet. The miso marinade will become dark brown and sticky.

Transfer the fish to a serving platter. Garnish with sliced green onions and serve immediately.

# Potato-Crusted Sea Bass with Chipotle Vinaigrette

Seafood alternatives: Bluefish, Pompano, Salmon

The stunning golden-crusted fish and spicy sauce make this dish a favorite for entertaining. Chipotle chiles are smoked jalapeños and are available canned in flavorful adobe sauce or dried. If using dried, simply reconstitute in warm water for 10 minutes. This dish is especially good served with sautéed hearty greens or steamed baby vegetables.

### Serves 4

4 (6 to 8-ounce) Chilean sea bass fillets

Salt

Freshly ground black pepper

1 pound russet potatoes, peeled and grated (about 2 cups)

3 tablespoons melted butter

1 tablespoon snipped fresh chives

Pat the fish dry and season lightly with salt and pepper.

Mix the potatoes with the butter and chives and season well with salt and pepper. Carefully spread an even layer of potatoes on each fillet. Chill the fish for at least 15 minutes to set the potato crust.

While the fish is chilling, make the vinaigrette. Heat the oil in a saucepan over medium high heat. Sauté the celery and onion until tender and aromatic, 3 to 4 minutes. Pour in the vinegar and reduce by half. Add the chile and tomato juice, and simmer for 5 minutes. Remove the sauce from the heat, cool slightly, and purée in a food processor or blender until smooth. Season with salt if needed.

## Chipotle Vinaigrette

1 teaspoon vegetable oil

1/4 cup diced celery

1/2 cup diced onion

3 tablespoons red wine vinegar

1 chipotle chile, chopped

1 1/2 cups tomato juice

Salt (optional)


2 to 3 tablespoons vegetable oil

Preheat the oven to 400°.

Heat a large, ovenproof skillet over medium heat. Swirl in the vegetable oil and carefully place the fish fillets, potato-side down in the skillet. Do not fuss with the fish until the potatoes form a crispy crust or the potatoes will stick and break up. Cook the fish until the potatoes are golden brown, about 10 minutes. Use a large spatula and carefully turn over the fish and potatoes. Place the skillet in the oven to finish cooking the fish, about 5 minutes.

Serve the crispy fish fillets over a spoonful of warm sauce. Serve additional sauce alongside.

# Mom, the Hunter-Gatherer

 I MADE CLAM CHOWDER the other night using my mother's recipe. Salt pork instead of bacon, of course, and no thickeners (or heavy cream). On the West Coast, where I now live, they like their clam chowder thick enough to float a fork—with a dash of sand. But I stand by my Boston roots when it comes to clam chowder.

Of course, it didn't taste as good as when she made it—something "in between" the ingredients was missing—but it was close enough to trigger some clam flashbacks, such as the first time I went clam digging. It was in Newport, Rhode Island, during World War II. One morning my mother and I and our downstairs neighbor, Millie, clambered into our 1939 Willys and went off to the coast in a clutter of buckets and clam shovels.

At the seashore, we changed into our bathing suits and headed out across the flats as the last of the tide receded, uncovering a phantasmagoria of sea critters that I would never have imagined.

"These are periwinkles . . . good bait for tautog," said my mother, holding up a handful.

Tautog, a member of the wrasse family indigenous to the East Coast, were her specialty (the counterpart on the Pacific side would be the lingcod, also a member of the wrasse family). I remember fishing for them off the rocks along the Rhode Island coast—tied to my mother's waist with a rope. We'd hop from rock to rock (with her it was always "the far rock"), dodging waves until, finally, at the right spot at last, she'd bait her hook with a crab or periwinkle (whatever her womanly intuition told her) and fire it off the end of an 11-foot rod into the thundering surf.

"Watch out for the jellyfish—they sting!"

I should have listened. One day I touched a Portuguese man-of-war (blue and beautiful) and had to be taken to the hospital.

A small crab scurried into a patch of seaweed, but not fast enough to elude my mother. With lightning hands, she snatched it up by the back legs and held it out for my inspection.

"Good to eat, but this one's a girl," turning it over to show me the roe, then releasing it.

"How come they only eat the boy crabs?"

We walked across a patch of sand riddled with holes, when suddenly water started squirting in all directions. *Clams!*

We started digging. They were Little Necks, the very best to eat. We dug so many that day that our buckets couldn't hold them all, and my mother and Millie started stuffing them into the tops of their bathing suits. When the game warden came around checking for undersized clams, he gave them a long look, whether out of suspicion or admiration I don't know, but he didn't dare ask any questions. Which was a good thing because they had their answer ready: "*What* clams?"

It was my mother who introduced me to the ways (and wiles) of the hunter-gatherer. There weren't many men around in those days (all the dads were in the war), but with a mother like mine, who needed them? The only man I knew was Roy Rogers riding his horse, Trigger, at the Saturday morning movies, singing those corny cowboy songs. I can see him now tipping his hat back, the sign he was going to sing *another* song, the theater erupting into a snowstorm of popcorn and booing.

Moms did a lot of fishing and played a lot of baseball in those days—as well as building a lot of planes and ships.

But to get back to the clams, they were all the more a special treat because of rationing. About the only fresh food to be had was seafood—and not easily had at that. Apart from a fish peddler who came down our street every Friday hawking "fresh fish" from the back of his truck (leaving a smell that lasted into the following week), availability was limited.

All the more reason to share our luck! My mother was always having neighbors over for fish, crab, mussels, even lobster (which she would buy directly from the lobster boats). But I remember most the steamed clams, dipping them in broth, then melted butter . . . until there was nothing left but a giant pile of empty shells and the broth, which we downed with a final flourish of gratitude.

I saw my mother just the other day—more than 60 years after that first day on the clam flats. She was all excited about a new crab recipe. She had won a prize with it (a portable oven), and the recipe was used on a cooking show on television. "Wash your hands and put on an apron," she ordered.

So we sat at the kitchen table cracking crab and gossiping about my three brothers, all of whom became commercial fishermen (she told them when they were kids to keep their lines in the water—and they did), and I realized that the key to her cooking was very simple and had never changed over all these years: making people happy.

That's something I'd love to do with my writing—and, in this case, I can! Here's Mom's crab recipe.

# Mom's Barbecued Crab

This is a messy-fingers dish, so have plenty of paper towels on hand. A few good friends and a bucket of cold beers are all you need as accompaniments.

| Serves 6 |
| --- |

3 large Dungeness crabs, cooked, cleaned, and split

1/4 cup olive oil

2 onions, thinly sliced

1 1/2 cups tomato juice

1/3 cup sugar

Juice of 1/2 lemon

2 tablespoons red wine vinegar

2 tablespoons soy sauce

1 clove garlic, crushed

1 teaspoon paprika

1/2 teaspoon salt

1/4 teaspoon powdered ginger

Dash of Tabasco sauce

Partially crack the legs and bodies of the crabs, leaving the pieces intact. Spread the pieces in a large roasting pan and set aside.

Heat the olive oil in a large skillet. Add the onion and sauté until they begin to soften, 3 to 4 minutes. Add the remaining ingredients and simmer for 20 minutes. Strain, pressing gently to remove as much sauce as possible.

Preheat the broiler and set the rack 4 to 6 inches below the element.

Pour half of the barbecue sauce over the cracked crabs and stir to coat evenly. Broil the crabs for 5 minutes. Pour the remaining sauce over, stir the crabs carefully to coat, and broil until the crabs are heated through and the shells are lightly browned, 3 to 4 minutes longer.

# Mom's Clam Chowder

Restaurants seem to compete to see who can make the thickest, richest clam chowder. But those who grew up gathering clams know that it isn't the cream and butter that make a chowder good, but the flavor of fresh clams and clam nectar. No type of clam is specified because almost any clam will do. Large clams need to be cleaned and chopped.

### Makes 8 cups

3 pounds clams, well scrubbed

1 cup beer, white wine, or water

1/2 pound salt pork or bacon, diced

1 onion, diced

1 pound potatoes, peeled and diced

1/2 teaspoon dried thyme

Freshly ground black pepper

2 cups milk or half-and-half

Salt (optional)

Oyster crackers or saltines

Place the clams and the beer in a large pot over medium-high heat. Steam the clams until they open, 6 to 8 minutes. Discard any clams that remain tightly closed. Strain off the flavorful nectar and pass it through a fine sieve to remove any grit or shell. Add water or additional clam nectar to the liquid to make 6 cups. Remove the clam meat from the shells. If you are using small clams, keep them whole. For larger clams, discard the stomachs and chop the meat. Keep refrigerated until ready to use.

In a soup pot, fry the salt pork until it is crisp and brown, 6 to 8 minutes. Pour off the excess fat. Add the onion and cook with the salt pork until they are translucent, 2 to 3 minutes. Stir in the clam nectar and potatoes. Season with thyme and black pepper. Simmer until the potatoes are tender, 25 to 30 minutes. Add the clam meat and milk and season with salt if needed.

Serve hot with crackers.

# Stripers!

*A gallant fish and a bold biter.*
—Frank Forester

FOR SOME, THE FIRST SIGNS OF SPRING can mean only one thing—stripers! In May, striped bass begin their annual migration from Chesapeake Bay, their main wintering grounds, to as far north as Canada's Gulf of St. Lawrence. They congregate in greatest numbers off Massachusetts, New York, and New Jersey, where they are greeted by thousands of worshippers who gather along the beaches with long wands (the instruments of their religion), casting offerings to the sacred fish.

Striped bass, *Morone saxatilis,* have been a New England tradition since colonial times. What was food to the pilgrims is now the most popular saltwater sport fish on the East Coast, based on what sportsmen spend in their pursuit, which, in the case of the striper, runs into millions of dollars. An average striper fisherman might easily spend upward of a thousand dollars on equipment alone (not including a dune buggy) before he even gets his worm in the water.

And, of course, you need a job geared to the phases of the moon. The tide table is the bass fisherman's clock and bible. On the incoming tide, he never misses a chance to fish, especially at night when the bass come right into the surf—and on the outgoing, he sleeps. A solitary life, you might say, but a strong camaraderie exists among striper fishermen. I've felt it myself, standing there on the beach in the dark, all alone, united by the sound of the surf and a shared sense of insanity.

Many have been smitten. The Roman scholar Pliny the Elder praised bass, preferring the ones taken in rivers, although he was probably referring to their culinary qualities not their piscatorial prowess (he was Italian, after all). The stripers' European cousin, *Dicentrarchus labrax* (known as *loup* or *bar* in France), is one of the most esteemed eating fish in Europe.

Former secretary of state Daniel Webster was a bass buff. He used to trot down from The Hill in his horse-drawn buggy and fly-fish for them on the Potomac River. Presidents Grover Cleveland and Teddy Roosevelt fished the same spot (near what is now the Chain Bridge).

Like salmon, stripers are an *anadromous* species, returning to freshwater (or at least brackish water) to spawn. When the Pilgrims first came to this country, the Potomac, Rappahannock, Roanoke, and Susquehanna rivers, to mention only a few, supported huge runs of spawning stripers. "I myselfe at the turning of the tyde have sene such multitudes . . . that one mighte go over their backs drishod," reported Captain John Smith of the Jamestown Colony.

Captain Smith was prone to exaggeration, but there are many similar accounts. Another was of 1,500 bass that were taken near Norfolk, Virginia, in a single set of the seine. According to an eyewitness, the bass weighed 75 to 85 pounds each.

Those poor Pilgrims. They ate turkey once a year—probably for penance—and the rest of the year they dined on *bar roti aux herbes* (sturgeon, salmon, oysters, scallops, crab, cod, and lobster), a seafood feast summed up by one William Wood, who, in 1634, claimed that the secret to catching striped bass was using lobster for bait.

Of course, the Pilgrims knew it wouldn't last, and in 1639, the Massachusetts Bay Colony ruled that neither bass nor cod could be used as fertilizer. Later, the colony taxed striped bass to support a "free school," the first public school in the New World.

By the time I got my line in the water, circa 1965, the striper population had fallen to a fraction of its former glory. I was teaching at a boys' boarding school in Vermont at the time, but during the summers I managed a yacht club on Cape Cod, where I dallied by day and fished by night.

I used saltwater worms for bait, creatures the size of garter snakes with legs like centipedes and a sharp bite if you weren't careful putting them on the hook. My revenge was casting them to the stripers. I'd stick my rod in a sand spike and stand for hours watching the tip of the rod against the moonlight, waiting for the slightest jiggle, the sign a striper was testing the bait.

Or I'd hurl plugs at an opaque horizon, running behind an outgoing wave in the dark as far as I dared to get a good cast, then trying to get back up the beach before the next one overtook me, which would mean standing in the cold, shivering.

Rarely did I catch a bass, but when I did, it was always a celebration. The smaller bass (less than 10 pounds) are the best to eat because the flesh is not as coarse as the larger fish. I prefer them baked Portuguese style with olive oil, smothered in onions and tomatoes. The flesh of the striper is white and moist, with a crablike taste.

To get back to the saga of the striper: The entire commercial catch in 1985 was less than 2 million pounds. In 1999, it was almost 7 million. From 1986 to 1990, striped bass fishing was banned or severely restricted from Massachusetts to North Carolina. The spawning estuaries were cleaned up and the result was an almost miraculous recovery. Today, biologists report seeing bass fingerlings in places they've never been seen before—proof that not every seafood resource is hell-bent for destruction. Oh yes, the saga of the striper has a happy ending—at least for now.

The West Coast is not to be left out of striper mania. Not only is it successfully farmed in California (a hybrid species), but wild stripers range from Washington's Columbia River to San Francisco Bay (the center of abundance) to as far south as Los Angeles. Stripers were introduced to the West Coast in 1886, when a truckload was driven across the country and dumped in the Pacific. Evidently, they liked the climate.

My advice is to purchase a whole striper (not more than five pounds) and bake it whole. Finding such a fish is not so difficult because there is now a flourishing business in cities across the country (wherever there's an Asian population) in live stripers (farmed hybrids). Just the right size, too. And here's some good advice from our Pilgrim forefathers. Keep the head:

"The Basse is . . . a delicate, fine fat fish, having a bone in its head, which contains a sawcerfull of marrow, sweet and good, pleasant to the pallat, and wholesome to the stomach" —William Wood, 1634.

# Striped Bass Roasted with Herbs
## (Lot roti aux herbes)

Seafood alternatives: Salmon, Bream, Cod, Snapper

This is an adaptation of a classic French recipe for spit-roasted fish. If you don't have a good rotisserie, just grill the fish over live coals. Otherwise, roast the fish on a rack in a hot oven. Cut a few deep slashes on each side so the heat can penetrate for more even cooking.

### Serves 2

1 striped bass (approximately 2 pounds), cleaned and scaled

1 tablespoon butter

1 teaspoon coarse salt (not rock salt)

$1/2$ teaspoon freshly ground black pepper plus more to taste

1 lemon, sliced

6 to 8 sprigs of whole fresh herbs (mint, rosemary, parsley, thyme, or bay leaves)

1 tablespoon olive oil

Salt

Preheat the oven to 500° or preheat an outdoor grill.

Clean the cavity of the fish thoroughly and pat dry with paper towels. Season the interior of the fish with the butter, coarse salt, $1/2$ teaspoon pepper, and a few slices of lemon. Place the whole herb sprigs into the cavity of the fish. Be generous, but pack the herbs loosely, so they don't insulate the interior of the fish. Seal the belly of the fish closed with skewers or bind with twine. Rub the exterior of the fish with olive oil and additional salt and pepper.

Place the fish on a rack in a roasting pan. Roast the fish until the skin is crispy and brown and the flesh is just opaque through, 15 to17 minutes. Or, grill the fish on a preheated grill for 8 minutes on one side, then flip and finish cooking for 6 to 7 minutes on the other side.

Carefully remove the fish to a platter lined with additional fresh herbs and lemon slices.

# Striped Bass Baked
# with Tomatoes and Onions

Seafood alternatives: Cod, Bluefish, Mackerel, Virtually Any Thick Whitefish

This is an easy preparation that suits almost any fish. The simple tomato sauce does not overpower the fillets and keeps the fish moist while cooking. Adjust the amount of crushed red chile flakes to your taste for a fiery or mild variation.

## Serves 6

4 tablespoons olive oil

2 cups thinly sliced onion

4 cloves garlic, sliced

1/4 teaspoon crushed red chile flakes

1 (14 1/2-ounce) can diced tomatoes or 2 cups peeled, seeded, and diced ripe tomatoes

1/2 cup dry white wine or dry sherry

1/2 teaspoon salt

1/2 teaspoon freshly ground pepper

2 pounds striped bass fillets

Lemon wedges for garnish

Chopped fresh parsley for garnish

Preheat the oven to 400°.

To make the sauce, cook the olive oil, onion, garlic, and red chile flakes in a saucepan over medium heat until the onion is tender, but not brown, about 10 minutes. Add the tomatoes and the wine, and season with salt and pepper. Simmer for 10 to 12 minutes until slightly thickened.

Place the fish in a lightly greased baking dish. Pour the sauce over the fish and bake for 12 to 15 minutes. The bass will be just opaque through. Very thick fillets will take longer.

Garnish with lemon wedges and parsley.

*Note:* If you are making this dish ahead of time, keep the sauce in the refrigerator until ready to use. Because the sauce will be cold when you bake the fish, add an additional 10 to 12 minutes of baking time to the total.

# The Geoduck Is a Sly Creature

 THINK OF THE MANY REGIONAL SEAFOODS we enjoy: crawfish from Louisiana, catfish from Mississippi, rainbow trout from Idaho, lobster from Maine, walleye from Minnesota, wild salmon from Alaska, and so on. But have you ever wondered about the regional seafood we *don't* enjoy? The seafood that we don't, for whatever reason, even know about?

Take my own region, the Pacific Northwest. You know it for its salmon and halibut, its fine oysters and cultured mussels. But have you ever heard of *lutefisk?* To anyone but a Scandinavian, this is a fish straight from hell. One taste of it will take away a layer of skin. Why would anyone soak a codfish in lye and then eat it? My theory is that the Vikings invented lutefisk to torture their enemies. *("No, no, anything but the lutefisk!")* After so many hits on the helmet, they started eating it themselves. No disrespect to Norwegians, of course. I live in a part of Seattle called "Little Norway" (a speck of green in a sea of Scandinavians), and I know how they can't stay away from the lutefisk. I see bumper stickers all around town: "Say No to Lutefisk!" Some regional secrets are best left kept.

A better example is the glorious geoduck, *Panope generosa.* Here's a Northwest delicacy that even people in the Northwest don't know about. Production is limited to Washington and British Columbia, and virtually all of it is exported to Asia where, in Hong Kong, a single geoduck will sell for as much as one hundred dollars.

But what is it? Geoduck (pronounced "gooey duck") is a large clam with a long siphon. The siphon, which measures up to 18 inches in repose and up to four feet fully extended, is often viewed as an object of mirth: a big clam that forgot to zip up its fly.

But the geoduck is more than a comical clam. It's a very savory one as well. The neck and breast meat are the edible parts. These are usually sold separately (the neck for sashimi, the breast for a variety of preparations from fritters to fried). Fresh is best, but don't flinch at frozen; the quality is excellent.

Geoduck is available year-round, mainly in Asian markets where they know the critter for the delicacy it is. And don't shy away from live geoduck. They're easy to clean. Scald them just enough to loosen the skin from the neck (no more than a minute), then plunge them into cold water. Remove the skin, discard the stomach and intestines, and rinse the rest. The recovery on necks (from total body weight) is about 20 percent; breasts 15 percent.

The necks (mild and somewhat crunchy) are excellent served raw or in quick-cooking stir-fry dishes. The breast meat has more flavor, a wonderful clammy taste perfect for chowders or fritters. If the geoduck is properly cared for, no tenderizing is necessary. (It will turn tough if overcooked, though.)

Despite the geoduck's macho image, they are shy, gentle creatures, spending their long lives (exceeding 100 years: The oldest geoduck on record was 146 years old) three or four feet under the sand. In fact, no one even knew geoducks existed until the 1950s, when some Navy divers noticed them on the bottom of Puget Sound while they were looking for a bomb. A commercial fishery started in 1970.

The geoduck has a small but fervid following. One group of admirers was so fond of the geoduck that it tried to make it the official state "bird." Evergreen State College in Olympia adopted the geoduck as its official mascot, although the college's athletic teams refused the title of "Fighting Geoducks," apparently not wanting to be compared to a clam. Few clams have inspired so many, as in the song by R. Konzak and J. Elfendahl:*

*Oh, it takes a lot of luck*
*And a certain kind of pluck*
*To dig around the muck*
*Just to get a geoduck.*
*'Cause he doesn't have a front,*
*And he doesn't have a back,*
*He doesn't know Donald*
*And he doesn't go quack!*

So much for the bad and the ugly of Pacific Northwest seafood. I'd tell you more about the "good," but I'd get in trouble if I gave away too many secrets. Whenever a regional seafood is "discovered," two things happen. It disappears from the local market and the price goes through the roof. My lips are sealed, but I'll whisper just two: *Mediterranean mussels* and *Kumamoto oysters.*

Mediterranean mussels were "discovered" on the West Coast only a few years ago. That is, they were mistaken for years for the familiar blue mussel, *Mytilis edulis,* when, in fact, they were *Mytilis galloprovincialis,* the famous mussel of Spain. Apparently they were introduced to the Northwest accidentally when a vessel from the Mediterranean, probably from Spain, left a few specimens behind. Mediterranean mussels, as they're now called, are being farmed in Washington's South Puget Sound with wild crops extending as far south as San Francisco Bay. Mediterranean mussels are similar to our blue mussels, with the singular difference that they spawn in the winter instead of the summer, and are therefore in prime condition when blues are out of season. The other thing about them is that they grow much larger than blue mussels—very suitable for a wider range of preparations: baked, barbecued, and in stews. This is the beloved mussel of Spain, so ransack your Spanish cookbooks for ideas.

The Kumamoto oyster is a "secret" that's pretty much out of the bag. They're a small, deep-shelled oyster ideal on the half shell. A subspecies of the Pacific oyster,

*From "The Gooeyduck Song," copyright 1972 by R. Konzak and J. Elfendahl.

**The Geoduck Is a Sly Creature**

Kumamotos are named after a bay in Japan (where they no longer exist). Nowadays you have to go to the Pacific Northwest to find them in any abundance.

So, sniff around your own region. No telling what you might find. And if you happen to be out my way, in "Little Norway," ask anyone on the street if they have any lutefisk to give away. You won't be disappointed. If it's geoduck you're looking for, you can always find it at Pike Place Market in Seattle, but try not to snigger when you see it. People are sensitive about their geoduck out here. Otherwise, try any Asian market in your own area. If they don't speak English, just describe what the geoduck looks like with your hands. Hopefully, they'll know what you mean. Remember, "It takes a certain kind of pluck . . . to eat a geoduck."

# Geoduck Sautéed in Butter, Japanese Style

Seafood alternatives: Razor Clams, Lobster, Scallops

In most sushi bars, the chefs will suggest you try the geoduck raw. It is sweet and kind of crunchy and quite delicious. But if you want a real treat, try a geoduck *bata yaki* (Japanese style)—sautéed in butter. This richness is found in very few ingredients, so a little goes a long way.

The belly meat of the geoduck is melt-in-your-mouth tender, but the neck is often tough. Some geoduck aficionados use only belly meat in dishes such as this and save the necks to be ground for fritters or chowder.

### Serves 4 as an appetizer

4 dried shiitake mushrooms

1/2 cup boiling water

1 live geoduck (about 2 pounds)

1/4 cup flour

3 tablespoons butter

4 cups baby spinach leaves, loosely packed

2 tablespoons sake

1 tablespoon soy sauce

1 green onion, sliced

Place the mushrooms in a small bowl with the boiling water, cover, and let reconstitute until soft, about 5 minutes. Strain the mushrooms through a very fine sieve or coffee filter, reserving the soaking liquid. Remove the stems from the mushrooms and discard. Slice the mushrooms and set aside.

To clean the geoduck, plunge the whole clam into boiling water for 5 seconds. Remove from the water and place in an ice bath. Slide a sharp knife along the edge of the clam and cut the shell away. Discard everything but the belly meat and neck. Peel off the coarse skin. (The dark skin should easily peel and rub off from the blanching. If it does not, blanch a few seconds more.) Slice the geoduck into bite-sized pieces and toss in the flour. Shake off any excess flour.

Melt 1 tablespoon of the butter in a large skillet or wok over high heat. Sear the geoduck until the outside is just golden brown, about 2 minutes. Add the mushrooms, spinach, sake, and soy sauce and stir-fry another minute. Lift out the ingredients with a slotted spoon onto a platter and return the pan to the heat. Pour in the mushroom water and reduce slightly. Whisk in the remaining butter. Add the green onion and pour the sauce over the geoduck.

Serve immediately.

# Crabs, Crabs, Crabs

CRABS—FASCINATING TO STUDY, even better to eat! I remember my first encounter with a crab: *Cancer irroratus*. It was on a dock in Newport, Rhode Island, circa 1947. I was dangling a fish head in the water, watching it for hours staring back up at me with glassy eyes, imagining a striped bass or big tautog engulfing it in its mouth—or maybe one of those exotic fish I read about in books, with high fins and a sharp bill—riding it out to sea, lifejacket strapped securely around me (worn at all times to please my mother), subduing it at last, and taking it home for dinner.

But the big one never came. Even small fish disdained my tactics, the big hook, the heavy twine. I was shunned by every creature in the sea—but one. And there he was, scuttling across the rocky bottom with reckless abandon, drawn inexorably by the smell of my bait, pouncing upon it with gusto, hanging on with both claws even as I lifted him out of the water and dropped him into the bucket, still holding on.

In a world where conviction changes with every political wind, crabs are an inspiration. When J. Alfred Prufrock in T. S. Eliot's famous poem searched for an image of certainty in a world of doubt, he turned to the crab "scuttling across the floors of silent seas."

Crabs don't mess around. Take, for example, the Alaska king crabs. Each spring, they march up the continental slope of the Bering Sea like hordes of Visigoths vanquishing everything in their path—starfish, sand worms, sea urchins, clams, one another. Larger ones can weigh as much as 20 pounds, with leg spans of more than five feet: giant armored spiders by the look of them. The smaller ones will sometimes travel in "domes," as many as a thousand stacked 40 feet high and 60 feet wide, scampering down the front and up the back in a veritable vortex of crab. Biologists call it a "defense mechanism"; I call it a lot of Crab Louies.

Crabs are not only great fighters, but great lovers. For example, the female king crab has to shed her shell (molt) before mating. To help her do it, the male clasps her by the claws and around the sea floor they go, literally dancing her out of her skin. This may take hours, at speeds scuba divers can't keep up with, culminating finally in the emergence of the female, soft and lovely in her new shell, a ragged Aphrodite.

Blue crabs do a similar underwater waltz. The male carries the female underneath him for several days until she's ready to molt (what watermen in Chesapeake Bay call "buck and rider"). The male, meanwhile, searches for a place to build her a house, of eel grass or even an old shoe, to protect her after her molt. The dance, the house . . . and now they mate—for six to 12 hours—and then the male moves on to his next dancing partner.

As fascinating as crabs are in the water, they are even more fun on the plate. I watch them, I admire them, I eat them. A crab would understand that. Crabs, I strongly suspect, are the most sought after seafood in the world—but not the most available. Luckily, we in North America are blessed with a variety and abundance unrivaled anywhere in the world. Here are some of the more delectable varieties, starting with Alaska and working our way around the country.

King crab is our largest—and most dramatic—crab, harvested in Alaska with an increasing amount coming from Russia. The crabs are captured live in baited pots (the old fish-head trick) under a strict management system.

There are three species of king crab on the market—red, blue, and golden—with red crab (larger and meatier) by far the preferred. King crab is available year-round as frozen cooked crab legs and claws—all in the shell. A word about "split claws." This is a product more common with snow crab, but it's also available for king. Called "snap and eat," the claws are scored so that all you have to do is snap the shell off and pop the meat in your mouth. If you're serving them—or any form of king crab for that matter—to guests watch out for the stampede! King crab is so good I've heard people growling while they were eating it—or was that me?

King crabs come cooked and frozen, the most economical way to get them out of Alaska in prime condition. When you buy king crab, all you have to do is steam it for a few minutes—and, as I say, stand back! The shells are hard to crack, by the way (too flexible), so toss the hammer and nutcracker and use a pair of scissors. Much easier. The only hard part is writing the check. But no crab is cheap. If it's cheap, it's imitation crab.

Don't confuse king crab with snow crab. King crab is sold primarily as legs and claws, while snow crab is sold in sections. Snow crab is smaller, cheaper—and very delicious. There are two sizes: the larger bairdi (a reference to its Latin name) and opilio. Bairdi is more expensive than the smaller opilio, the latter sometimes referred to as "blue-collar" crab because it's cheaper and often a bargain at all-you-can-eat crab fests. To me, both taste just as good as king crab, but lack the dramatic presentation of the larger, leggier king.

The Dungeness crab is one of the tastier crabs in the ocean, harvested from Kodiak, Alaska, to northern California. Unlike its bigger brethren from the Bering Sea, it's available live when in season (December and January are the big months) and year-round as frozen whole cooked crab or as frozen meat. Split claws are also a popular item.

Dungeness (back removed) are normally served cold as "cracked crab." That is, someone has done you the favor of cracking the shell so you can remove the meat daintily; otherwise, you'll need a hammer or nutcracker (or a good set of teeth) to get it out of the shell. In either case, put on a bib. It's part of the ritual and you'll probably need it.

When you buy Dungeness crab from your fish market, the carapace (back) should be removed by your dealer when you purchase it, although it's easy enough to do yourself—simply pull it away from the body—but messy.

Dungeness is the ultimate crabmeat for salads: tender and very tasty, visually pleasing. Fresh is best, but frozen is far more available. Don't try to pick it from the shell yourself unless you have plenty of time.

Skipping across the country to New England, we are now in lobster ("lobstah") country, not a bad crustacean, but there are crabs here, too. The rock crab and the Jonah crab are the main ones: both are processed mainly as meat, although there is a growing market for Jonah crab claws. The crabs are generally too small to serve whole, but I can remember as a kid in Boston eating them fresh from the carts in Haymarket Square. The meat is excellent, much cheaper than Dungeness (but not quite as tasty). Both the meat and the claws are available year-round frozen. If you buy the claws, be ready to do some hammering.

Farther down the coast it's the blue, the beloved crab of the mid-Atlantic to as far south as the Gulf of Mexico. Blues are mainly sold live or as crabmeat. Smallish in size, they're anything but fast food.

For the uninitiated, soft-shells can be a bit of a challenge because they're consumed shell and all—that is, just after they molt. I remember my first time. I was doing a story on a seafood company in Sarasota, and one day my host took me to a "special place" for lunch, deep within the mangrove swamps. For a while I was worried that he didn't like the way the story was going. "A smuggler's den," he called it, which, as it turned out, had been true at one time. The smugglers, however, had all turned to crabbing.

Inside, I looked down the bar sizing up the patrons and quickly ordered a whiskey. My host, meanwhile, ordered lunch. It arrived on a small plate, a bun with crab legs sticking out all around it. Every eye in the place was on me. I downed the whiskey and bit into it, *crunch, crunch,* and . . . and . . . it was fabulous!

A crab po' boy—that's what they call this sandwich. I ate a lot of them in Florida and Louisiana.

As I mentioned earlier, blue crabs are soft just after they molt, almost melting in your mouth. There are many ways of preparing them (Baltimore being the culinary capital), all relatively simple. You can buy them frozen, ready to eat, no cracking or hammering—just dab them in a little coating and fry 'em up and you're off to crab heaven.

Florida is a crab-lover's paradise. Stone crab claws top the list here. Joe's Stone Crab House in Miami Beach is legendary, the place to go if you can survive hours of waiting in line. Only the claws of the stone crab are eaten (the rest of the crab is released to grow another claw—a "renewable resource"). The claws are a snap to eat, just crack and dunk. A regional delicacy, but very available over the Internet. The season for fresh is mid-October to mid-May, but you can now buy them frozen year-round.

Golden crab is Florida's version of an Alaska snow crab, a big gangly crab that is a relative newcomer to the commercial fishery. It's a deepwater species harvested on both sides of the state. I spent five days on a golden crab boat out of Key West once. It's a very clean fishery (virtually no bycatch, only golden crab coming up in the pots), and the resource appears to be strong. During the trip, I sampled the crab thoroughly (as I always feel professionally obliged to do) and am a big fan of the species. Goldies are frozen in the same product forms as Alaska snow crab (for which it is sometimes substituted in years when the Alaska catch is down), but mainly they're sold fresh on the local market, particularly in the Miami and Fort Lauderdale area.

And, of course, there are crabs from all around the world: the glorious mudcrab (Australia and southeast Asia), a delicacy masked by its humble name; the coconut crab (Indo-Pacific), largest of the land crabs weighing up to eight pounds, feeding on coconuts and small animals, another delicacy (steam it in coconut milk); the Tasmanian king crab, flesh as white as snow—I love them all. Crabs have character, conviction, and, above all, they are creatures of consummate good taste.

# Dungeness Crab Club Sandwiches

Seafood alternatives: Bay Shrimp; Any Cooked, Flaked Fish

Delightfully decadent! You may never go back to turkey and ham after you've tasted this triple-decker sandwich layered with sourdough toast, crab, and pancetta.

## Serves 4

1/2 pound fresh Dungeness crab-meat, picked over to remove any bits of shell or membrane

1/2 cup mayonnaise

1 teaspoon minced fresh chives

1 teaspoon grated lemon zest, or 1 tablespoon freshly squeezed lemon juice

Dash of Tabasco sauce

12 slices sourdough bread, toasted

4 leaves crisp green lettuce, rinsed and dried

8 thin slices ripe tomato

8 slices pancetta or bacon, fried crisp

1 ripe avocado, peeled, pitted, and sliced (optional)

Freshly ground black pepper

In a medium bowl, combine the crabmeat, half the mayonnaise, chives, lemon zest, and Tabasco sauce. Stir to mix.

To assemble the sandwiches, divide the crab mixture evenly on 4 slices of the toast. Spread 4 slices of toast with the remaining mayonnaise. Arrange them, mayonnaise side up, on the crab. Top with the lettuce, two slices each of the tomato and pancetta, and avocado. Season with plenty of black pepper and top with the remaining toast slices. Press down gently on the sandwiches and cut them into 4 diamonds, securing each section with a fancy toothpick if the whim strikes you. Serve immediately.

# Panfried Soft-Shell Crab with Roasted Garlic and Pepper Vinaigrette

Seafood alternatives: Calamari Rings

The fresh soft-shell crab season is fleeting. If you can't wait for the crispy live crab to show up at your favorite market, a good frozen product is an acceptable substitute.

---

### Serves 4

### Vinaigrette

1 red bell pepper, seeded

1 yellow bell pepper, seeded

1 small onion, quartered, or 2 peeled shallots

10 to 12 large cloves garlic, peeled

$1/2$ cup olive oil

2 tablespoons sherry vinegar (or a good-quality malt or red wine vinegar)

2 tablespoons freshly squeezed lemon juice

1 tablespoon chopped fresh parsley

1 teaspoon chopped fresh oregano

$1/2$ teaspoon salt

$1/2$ teaspoon freshly ground black pepper

Preheat the oven to 450°.

To make the vinaigrette, cut the peppers into large chunks. Place the peppers, onion, garlic, and olive oil in a baking pan or an ovenproof skillet and roast in the oven, turning the vegetables occasionally until the garlic is tender and the peppers and onion have browned, about 30 minutes.

Let the vegetables cool slightly, and then pour the mixture into the bowl of a food processor or blender. Add the vinegar, lemon juice, parsley, oregano, salt, and pepper, and pulse until evenly mixed but not perfectly smooth. Set the sauce aside, or keep in the refrigerator in an airtight container for up to 2 weeks. Warm just before serving.

8 soft-shell crabs

3/4 cup flour

1 teaspoon salt

1 teaspoon freshly ground
black pepper

Pinch of paprika

Light olive oil for frying

Herb sprigs for garnish

To clean the soft-shell crab, lift up each side of the soft shell and remove the lungs. Use scissors to snip off about $1/4$ inch of the front shell and the eyes, and discard. Mix together the flour with the salt, pepper, and paprika. Dredge the crab in the seasoned flour and shake off the excess.

Heat a few tablespoons of the oil in a skillet over medium-high heat. Carefully place 2 or 3 crabs, top-shell down, in the hot oil and stand back! Soft-shell crabs often crackle and pop sending hot oil flying! Cook the crabs until they are crisp and golden brown, about 2 minutes, then flip and finish cooking on the other side, 2 to 3 minutes more. Remove the crabs and drain lightly on crumpled paper towels. Repeat with the remaining crabs.

To serve, gently toss the crisp crabs in the warm vinaigrette. Garnish with herb sprigs. Serve the remaining sauce alongside for dipping.

# No-Frills Fish

I'VE BEEN LOOKING AT SOME of these new-fangled fish gadgets—you know, the ones that make everything "simple." Like those expensive pans in the shape of a fish. Or twenty-dollar oyster shuckers that don't work (Julia Child recommends an old-fashioned can opener that sells for less than $1). Copper-bottom fish poachers that sell for an arm and a leg.

Sorry, but I like to travel light when it comes to seafood. All you really need is a good filleting knife, a pair of needle-nose pliers to pluck out bones, and a nutcracker for crab. A scaler would be nice, but a knife will work just as well.

Besides, I can't afford all those fancy gadgets. You've heard of the Frugal Gourmet? Well, I'm the Destitute Gourmet. No panoply of pots and pans (and TV cameras) in my kitchen. In fact, I don't even need a kitchen—that's how easy seafood is to prepare. All I need to produce a great seafood dinner is a sharp knife, some matches—and a generous expense account.

Of course, I'm kidding about the expense account. It's just that the idea of a simple seafood dinner reminded me of a trip I took to Mexico some years back. Nick Vitalich and David Ptak of Chesapeake Fish Company in San Diego invited me to visit their fish camps on the Baja Peninsula. Chesapeake supplies some of California's most upscale restaurants with seafood—and has been doing so since the turn of the century. If you order the *baquetta,* an exquisite gourmet grouper at, say, San Diego's famous Star of the Sea restaurant, chances are it was trucked across the border in one of Chesapeake's trucks.

"It's a story that has to be done," I told my publisher. He nodded his blessing, and out the door I went. He always liked it best when I was gone, a powerful synergy that worked well for both of us for more than twenty years.

The occasion was Chesapeake's annual goodwill tour of its 35 or so fish camps strung out along the Baja Peninsula: a time to iron out any problems with fishermen, give them a pat on the back and a Chesapeake hat.

So, off we went in Ptak's camper, bound for the Baja Peninsula, a slender finger of land that pokes some 800 miles into the Pacific, surrounded on both sides by some of the richest fishing grounds in the world. Vitalich and Ptak had been going down there for many years. Ptak and his wife, Sally, used to drive down there when the highway was not much more than a coyote trail, totally lacking in roadside amenities. When it would rain, they'd step out of the truck, strip down, and take a shower in the middle of the road. Vitalich's family has been buying fish from there for three generations—ever since his grandfather came to California from an island in the Adriatica and started the company.

Our first stop was *Laguna Manuela,* a fish camp on the Pacific side. A crowd of fishermen gathered around our truck: "How is your father, friend of my father? And your grandfather, friend of my grandfather?" and so on, all in Spanish.

That's how it went from camp to camp, very cordial, but always a hidden agenda would slowly surface through the small talk. In *Laguna Manuela,* it was poor fish quality. Two of the last three shipments to San Diego had to be turned back. The fishermen were threatening to quit.

"Maybe you need more ice?" ventured Ptak.

"Maybe if we had a better truck," suggested the camp boss. Chesapeake had just bought a new truck for one of the other camps.

"And the 'Tiburones'? They are still winning?" asked Vitalich, wondering if he'd have to buy a new truck.

*"Sí! Sí!"*

The baseball team's victories were recounted with pride as we stood on the beach nodding and smiling. "Did you get the new uniforms I sent you?" asked Vitalich, a subtle reminder of past favors. Everyone was smiling now, edging closer to the sensitive questions. The price this year? The ice? The new truck?

And so it went, from camp to camp. How to describe one? A ramshackle collection of huts slapped together along the beach, nets draping from the tin roofs, fish drying on racks, and, depending on the time of day, *pangas* pulled up on the beach in front of the huts, the ubiquitous fishing boat of these parts: 20 feet long, equipped with Yamaha outboard motors. The camps ranged in size from several hundred fishermen to only a dozen or so. When the fishing got bad, the camp vanished overnight, reappearing the next day in some more likely spot. *Vagabundos,* as they were called in Spanish.

My story on Chesapeake was going great, but on the culinary front the situation was desperate. In the morning Vitalich had dry cereal and water for breakfast; Ptak jogged. Lunch was a can of tunafish on dry bread. And no restaurant in sight. I was starved for something to eat. I'm a food writer, I need food to write. Plus, my head was thumping from listening to Vitalich's Pavarotti tapes. By the fourth day, I was driven by two powerful passions: hunger and escape.

I prevailed on my hosts to let me run free for one night: to walk the beach, fish for my dinner, sleep under the stars. They dropped me off on a beach just outside of San Juanico, a small fishing village on the Pacific side.

Thus began my experiment in no-frills fish. Note that I have no cooking gear whatever. It always spoils the fishing, anyway; curdles the karma, as it were. I mean, you don't want the fish to see you coming. Besides, I'd have to pack it in. I didn't want to be like a fellow I knew who toted a cast-iron frying pan into the woods with him because he liked the smell of frying bacon in the morning. (I think he fell in a creek and sank to the bottom.)

So there I was on a trackless beach. No Winnebagos, no campgrounds, no sign of humanity. Only me and the beach—and an old dog from the village.

Time to catch a fish.

Wading into the surf, I edged a step closer to the horizon. *What if I step on a stingray?* Never mind. I know the big ones are always just out of reach (the lesson of Papa Hemingway), but I was drawn by the lure of the ocean, edging a step deeper.

I was using shrimp for bait. I recommend shrimp; if the fishing is poor, you can always eat the bait. Here's another tip: Always fish when you're hungry. It's the same principle as shopping on an empty stomach: You'll bag more fish.

Up to my waist now, I cast my baited hook to *los pescados:* groupers, snappers, and sea bass—but no *tiberones,* please. Sharks. I wanted to be *close* to the food chain, not *part* of it.

I tightened the slack on my line, waiting. I could already see—smell, hear—the fish sizzling on the fire, juicy and sweet, scooping out the succulent flesh with my seashell spoon until I could eat no more, then picking my teeth with their bones.

*A nibble!*

I set the hook, battling the fish to the beach. A California sea bass—*delicioso!*

And another! And another!

The Mexicans call them *corvina,* a favorite fish. I wrapped them in kelp, tossing them onto the coals, hissing and sputtering, then set the table, a driftwood plank for a plate, a pair of bleached fish bones for chop sticks . . .

The sun was setting now, only the last traces of blue in the sky. The sea was as flat as a tortilla, already sparkling with the lights of shrimp boats.

The fish—I almost forgot!

I lifted it out of the fire with makeshift tongs, eagerly unwrapping it. It looked perfect, slightly blackened but that's the latest trend. I peeled back the skin and sampled the ivory-white flesh. It tasted just like . . . *kelp.*

The next one I pierced with a stick and tried cooking over the fire like a hot dog. The stick broke and the fish burned.

One fish left. I wrapped it in aluminum foil, and it came out perfect. (Add the foil to the list.)

Later that night, dreaming of hamburgers in paradise, I felt something wet on my face. The dog from the village was licking me. I considered it a compliment.

The cost of that dinner (excluding airfare) was about a nickel a serving—and all the cooking utensils were disposable. No-frills fish is the way to go, only you don't have to catch it yourself. The supermarket will do just fine. One thing, though: Forget the kelp.

Back in the village the next morning, I sat down on a rock and started writing in my notebook. Soon Vitalich and Ptak would arrive, and my story would resume. And there *was* a story. They reminded me of the gypsies in Gabriel Garcia Marquez's *One-Hundred Years of Solitude* who carted a cake of ice across South America without letting it melt, only in their case it was fish. The chefs got the credit, but these gypsies were the real heroes.

I heard music in the wind . . . *"Vesta la giubba e la faccia . . ."* They were back, the missionaries of fresh fish. Time to go to work—and on a full stomach, too. No-frills fish, it works every time.

# "Emergency" Fried Oysters

It was the kind of emergency you can only hope for. We were camping on the beach with a valid shellfish permit and ran into an unexpected bounty of big, fresh Pacific oysters, the likes of which only the bravest will slurp raw. Unfortunately, we had a limited larder. The resulting recipe was crude and rather unattractive, but delicious. As campsite dinners go, it was one of the best.

**Serves 2 to 4**

2 dozen fresh oysters, shucked

1 cup finely crushed corn chips

2 to 3 tablespoons olive oil, butter, margarine, or bacon drippings

Tabasco sauce

Roll the oysters in the crushed chips and fry in the olive oil on a well-greased griddle over a campfire, turning once. Cook about 2 minutes total and serve hot off the grill with a good dash of Tabasco sauce.

# Fish on a Stick

If you have lounged on the beaches of Mexico, you may have seen children waving grilled fish on sticks for your dining pleasure. It is basic beach food. After purchasing your selected grilled fish, you are simply handed a bowl of salt, some slices of lime, and a bottle of hot sauce. If there are no young hucksters nearby, but you have a flame and a fish, try making this yourself. The trick is to rotate the fish only occasionally as it cooks, or it will fall into the fire just as it is done to perfection. Snapper, Pacific cod, small Striped bass, and tilapia are all excellent when cooked on a stick.

## Serves 1

1 fish, gutted and scaled

Salt

Pepper

Lime wedges for garnish

Hot pepper sauce for garnish

Sharpen a sturdy (nonpoisonous, please!) stick. Thread the stick through the mouth of the fish, and then pierce through the center meat of the tail. Secure the fish with twine (if you have it). Slash the sides of the fish with a sharp knife. Season with salt and pepper if you have it.

Cook the fish over hot, ash-covered coals, until the skin is dark and crispy and the flesh is opaque through. The fish eyes will be completely opaque and protruding when the fish is fully cooked. Eat with your fingers. Serve with lime wedges and hot pepper sauce if you have it.

# Steamed Clams with Bacon and Beer

If you are simmering this on a beach, people will come from miles around just to discover what smells so good! A light ale is a good choice here, but whatever happens to be in the cooler will work fine. If you don't drink beer, this recipe doesn't suffer too much when made with water or broth. Have plenty of crusty bread on hand for sopping up the cooking juices.

**Serves 4**

4 slices bacon, chopped

1 small onion, chopped

2 cloves garlic, chopped

3 pounds manila clams, scrubbed well

1 cup beer, water, or chicken broth

Fry the bacon in a medium pot until soft and golden, about 4 minutes. Add the onion and garlic and continue cooking until the bacon is nicely browned and the onion is tender, about 4 minutes longer. Stir in the clams and add the beer. Cover the pot and steam the clams for 6 to 7 minutes, until they open. Discard any clams that do not open. Stir gently to mix with the bacon, garlic, and onion, and serve immediately.

# The Raw Truth About Oysters

*I never met a man so brave as et an oyster.*
—Jonathan Swift

WHAT'S LIFE WITHOUT AN OYSTER? An empty shell. Oysters are like no other food. They impart a feeling of well-being and happiness—cure digestive problems, prod jaded appetites, persuade men of powers they didn't know they had. Oysters are the perfect marriage of man and mollusk. And of woman and mollusk. Venus, rising from the sea, popped out of an oyster.

Oysters spur us on to great feasts. Diamond Jim Brady, the legendary American financier, downed them by the dozens. The Romans so relished oysters they forced thousands of slaves to harvest them in the British Isles, transporting them live across the English Channel and over the Alps in snow-covered barrels. Emperor Vitellius power-supped on a thousand oysters at a sitting, according to his chroniclers.

And they spur us on to great sex. Cassanova loved oysters, calling them "a spur to love." According to historians, he ate 50 of them every morning before getting out of bed—or was it before getting into bed? "So delicate a morsel must be a sin in itself," he sighed.

What is this about oysters and making love? Do they make you feel sexy? I don't know. They make *me* feel sexy. The aphrodisiac qualities of oysters are probably more a matter of mind than mollusk, but the belief is deeply embedded in history. One theory is that oysters, because they are so nutritious, put you in the hum of health. Another is that they are a dark alchemy of minerals (including zinc) concocted by a very sexy Mother Nature.

Their reproductive habits only add fuel to their amatory reputation. During spawning season (usually July and August) half their body weight is devoted to reproduction, a single female releasing a half-billion eggs into the water. The first oyster to spawn triggers the others, until the water is milky with group spawning. Where egg and sperm collide, larvae are formed (if they all collided, the earth would be a solid bed of oysters).

After a few days, the free-swimming larvae develop feet and sink to the bottom, anchoring themselves to rocks or bits of oyster shell. The tiny seedlings are called *spat;* the material the spat collects on is called *cultch* and the entire process is called a *set*. A good set means lots of spat; a poor set means the opposite. Another thing about the sex lives of oysters is they like to change their sex, starting out as males, changing to females after a year or two, then switching back to males in later life.

Like mussels and clams, oysters are bivalves—a bivalve being a mollusk with two hinged shells. The shells (or valves) are controlled by a powerful adductor muscle, which is what makes shucking oysters a challenge. The adductor muscle must be severed before the soft body cradled between the shells (swaddled in a delicate liquor) is free to be slurped.

Oysters grow in brackish water, feeding on tiny plankton, which they filter through the water. A single oyster might siphon 20 to 40 gallons of water a day, which is why oysters are so susceptible to pollution. Hence, oysters (mussels and clams) can be sold legally only if they are harvested from beds certified by the National Shellfish Sanitation Program. If they're not certified, *don't* eat them.

How fast oysters grow to a marketable size depends on temperature: as fast as two years in the Gulf States where water temperatures are very warm, to as long as six years in the colder waters of New England and Canada. (You can tell an oyster's age by counting the ridges—or "shoots"—on its shell. Same as the trunk of a tree, each circle represents a season of growth.)

The old saw that oysters are only good to eat during the months with "r" in them (the months when oysters aren't spawning) is outdated. True, oysters turn themselves into a milky goo during spawning, but in these days of modern transportation, prime oysters are available year-round (from the colder waters of Canada or from Chile and Australia, where the seasons are opposite to ours). "All-season" oysters from the Pacific Northwest (so called "triploids" and "tetraploids") don't spawn at all, and are available year-round.

The real concern with eating oysters during the summer is safety, not taste. Oysters harvested from warmer waters, especially—and virtually exclusively—from the Gulf of Mexico, are susceptible to a bacterium called *Vibrio vulnificus,* which can be deadly in raw oysters ingested by persons with depressed immune systems or liver problems (the list of candidates is very long: cancer patients, AIDS victims, alcoholics, the elderly). According to the Centers for Disease Control, there's an average of 35 deaths annually from vibrio (all from Gulf oysters) and that's with only a few states reporting. No doubt the number is much higher. (California now requires a sign to be posted anywhere Gulf oysters are served raw, regardless of the time of year.) Personally, I'd never eat a Gulf oyster unless it was cooked. A cooked oyster is a safe oyster, but a raw oyster—that's safe—is a gift from above.

Don't let the ostraphiles baffle you with their oyster snobbery—all those names they have for oysters. There are only two major species of oysters in North America: the Atlantic (or Eastern) oyster, *Crassostrea virginica,* and the Pacific oyster, *Crassostrea gigas.* The two account for 98 percent of the national production.

But what about all those *other* names?

They refer to the different regions where oysters are grown. "Wescott Bays" refer to oysters grown in Wescott Bay in Washington State. "Chincoteagues" are an oyster from an island off Virginia. "Cape Cods" are from Wellfleet, Massachusetts. And so on.

Not that these names don't have meaning. Water quality, temperature, mineral content, salinity, and nutrients all vary from one oyster bed to the next (even within a bed), imbuing the oyster with subtle differences in taste and texture. (A good oyster tippler can tell you what side of the bed an oyster came from by the way it tastes—or so he'll tell you.) Words such as *briny, sweet, coppery, metallic, crisp, and clean* are typically used to describe the taste of oysters.

Oysters are sold mainly as shucked fresh meats or live in the shell. Both are wonderful. But if you're going to cook oysters, no sense in prying them out of their shells—buy them already shucked. But *don't* eat shucked oysters raw because a lot of Gulf oysters go to shucking houses. Your best bet is to cook them.

Ideally, eat raw oysters as they're shucked live from the shell. When you store them in the refrigerator, *don't* cover them with ice because the freshwater will kill them. And don't wrap them in plastic or they'll suffocate. One more thing: Oysters have a top and a bottom. Make sure you store them so the cupped side is facing upward or the liquor will spill out.

Happy tippling. And don't be put off by my cautionary tips. I can't write about eating raw oysters without warning consumers, especially because the FDA is doing such a poor job of it. Eating oysters has always been linked with love, and love has its dangers. Yet who can resist? As one tippler put it, eating raw oysters the first time is "the gastronomic equivalent of losing your virginity." And who can resist the Queen of Bivalves? Not us.

# Hangtown Strata

Hangtown fry is a classic dish of fried oysters and eggs from the Old West. This savory bread pudding is made with all of the flavors of the traditional preparation, but with a lot less fuss. If you make it the night before, you can drink your first cup of coffee while it bakes. If you like a crispy top, bake this in a shallow pan. If you prefer a rich and creamy center, bake it in a deep soufflé dish. This is a great way to use leftover bread!

### Serves 4 to 6

6 cups cubed crusty bread (crusts removed)

1 pint small, shucked fresh oysters

1/2 pound bacon, fried crisp and chopped

1 (10-ounce) box frozen spinach, thawed and squeezed dry

1 cup diced tomatoes

1 clove garlic, minced or pressed

1/2 teaspoon salt

1/2 teaspoon freshly ground black pepper

6 eggs

1 cup milk

1/2 teaspoon dry mustard

1/4 teaspoon ground cayenne pepper

Lightly grease a 2-quart casserole or 9 by 13-inch baking pan.

In a large bowl, gently toss the bread cubes with the oysters, bacon, spinach, tomatoes, garlic, salt, and pepper. Place the bread mixture into the prepared dish. Whisk together the eggs, milk, mustard, and cayenne. Pour the egg mixture evenly over the ingredients in the casserole dish. Cover and let rest in the refrigerator overnight.

Preheat the oven to 400°.

Bake the strata uncovered in the oven until the strata is brown and crisp on the top and along the sides and the eggs are just set, 25 to 30 minutes. Let the strata rest for 5 minutes before serving.

# Oyster and Stout Pie

Oysters and a splash of good Irish ale enliven this version of a classic potpie. Use your favorite unsweetened pie crust or frozen puff pastry for the top. Or, as a variation of shepherd's pie, top the dish with mashed potatoes. If you don't have homemade beef stock, Knorr makes a good-quality concentrated liquid beef stock that can be made strong without being too salty.

### Serves 4 to 6

2 cups peeled and diced potato

1$^1$/2 cups peeled and diced carrot

1 cup diced onion

$^3$/4 cup diced celery

4 tablespoons flour

1 teaspoon salt plus more to taste

$^1$/2 teaspoon freshly ground black pepper plus more to taste

1 pint shucked fresh small oysters (or large oysters, halved)

1 cup strong beef or veal stock

$^1$/2 cup Guinness or other stout ale

1 teaspoon horseradish

2 tablespoons butter or margarine

1 recipe of your favorite pastry (shortcrust, puff pastry, biscuit dough, or mashed potato)

Preheat the oven to 375º. Lightly butter a deep-dish pie pan or gratin dish.

In a bowl, toss together the potato, carrot, onion, celery, flour, 1 teaspoon salt, and $^1$/2 teaspoon pepper. Pour the vegetables into the prepared dish. Top with the oysters.

Stir together the stock, stout, and horseradish. Pour the mixture over the oysters and vegetables and dot with butter. Cover with the pastry. Cut air vents into the top of the pastry. Brush with water and sprinkle with salt and black pepper to taste.

Bake the pie for 1 hour. The center of the pie will bubble and the vegetables will be tender. Let rest for 5 minutes before serving. Serve warm.

# Follow Your Fish

THE PERSON WHO INFLUENCED MY COOKING the most is Alan Watts, the Zen master and religious mystic. I used to listen to his tapes in the kitchen back in the 1960s while I was throwing together yin and yang for dinner. One day he talked about the Zen of making coffee. A mundane subject for a mystic, I thought, but Watts was one who could see a world in a grain of coffee. "Why measure the grounds before brewing it?" asked the great teacher.

"To get a better cup of coffee?"

But I was too square. I lacked coffee karma—which, for all I knew, was a flavor of ice cream. The idea behind Watts' coffee-pot philosophy, I realized, was not to be bound by conventional formulas. In other words: *follow your fish.*

So, forget the old standbys when it comes to seafood entertaining. Bury the smoked mussels and oysters, and try something new like . . . cod tongues. Now here's an appetizer that will loosen up conversation. Your guests will love it, especially if you don't tell them what it is (just make up a Norwegian name, something like *fer-skalangenlingen,* and wink).

Actually, cod tongues are as American as clam chowder. In the days of the New England cod schooners, dory fishermen kept track of their catches by cutting out the tongues and stringing them on a wire. After they were tallied at the end of the day, they were salted in barrels and later sold as a delicacy. Wonderful to eat, easy to prepare (just dip them in egg and milk and sauté for two to three minutes)—but not so easy to find. Cod tongues are located in cod heads, which are usually discarded or exported to Norway.

Once you locate a source for cod heads, you have some additional options. The heads themselves make an excellent chowder, plus the "cheeks" (meaty morsels located just behind the gill plates) can be served with the tongues for Tongues and Cheeks (one of my favorite dishes).

Cod eyes are another possibility. Although I've never eaten them, I'm sure they're very good (seagulls love them). I have eaten salmon eyes (very savory), although the pupils are quite hard, putting you at risk of losing a filling or a tooth (the best method is to eat them like oysters, swirling them around gently in your mouth before swallowing). The Japanese love fish eyes, preferring those of the bigeye tuna *(mebachi)*; the size of a small apple, they may be more than a mouthful for most Westerners.

Seafood has so many possibilities it's a shame not to flaunt them. What about eels? Excellent choice! Eels are a traditional delicacy in Europe dating back centuries—and in Early America as well. In colonial New England, the city fathers of Gloucester, Massachusetts, were under an edict to ship eels to England every Christmas, to be savored by his majesty's subjects. Back then, there were so many eels along the East Coast you could slip across the rivers on 'em.

The life cycle of eels is one of the most romantic in all of nature. By the millions, eels enter the rivers along the Eastern seaboard in the spring after a journey of more than a year. Once in the river, the males and females separate, the females migrating far upriver, through rapids and over waterfalls, while the males laze around in the lower river, waiting. Twelve years they wait.

Then, one moonlit evening, the females swim downriver joining the males at the mouth. The males are wearing black for the occasion (perhaps in anticipation of their death) and, together, they swarm out of the river for a fling in the Sargasso Sea. They love, they die. And they are eaten. In December, they're captured from the

St. Lawrence River to Chesapeake Bay and delivered live in aerated tanks to major eastern cities. Fried, baked, sautéed, jellied, or smoked, they are superb. And inspirational if you're interested in getting slimmer.

One of my favorite candlelight dinners is Eel for Two. Very elegant, very sexy. For this occasion I recommend only live eels. They're a lot more fun—and more easily obtained than you might think (the hard part is finding a date).

And here's the best part. Getting a grip on a live eel is just about impossible. The simplest method is to release the eel in a bucket of rock salt. The rock salt will kill the eel while, at the same time, de-sliming it. The next step is to skin it. To do this, nail the head to a board, make an incision around the neck (just behind the gills), and then, with a pair of pliers, peel off the skin with one quick pull.

How your date reacts to this will be a good test of how the evening is going. Fainting is not necessarily a bad sign and could be merely from too much excitement. On the other hand, if your date slips out the door while you're skinning the eel—or dials 911—no problem. Just remember, the eel is celibate for 12 years.

So, next time you're preparing seafood for a special occasion, remember: *Follow your fish.* The ocean is filled with rare delicacies that your guests would surely be thrilled to try. Here are just a few suggestions:

**SEA URCHIN ROE.** California and Maine are major producers, the two primary ports being Oxnard and Portland, respectively. Shop Japanese markets to find this very savory delight. To sample, try any good sushi bar; it's called *uni.*

**SALMON CAVIAR.** The best is from chum salmon called *ikura,* available through most caviar dealers—or direct from a salmon processor (almost any in Alaska). Don't confuse salmon caviar with the salmon eggs you use for bait! And, no, it doesn't taste or smell fishy at all. Serve with crackers and cream cheese.

**HALIBUT CHEEKS**. Available through your fish market, probably on special order. Fresh is best. Serve them lightly sautéed in butter wedges of lemon on the side.

**FLYINGFISH ROE** (called *tobiko* in Japanese). Not to be consumed by itself, but as a tasty and colorful (fluorescent orange) garnish on salads. Go to Japanese markets for this one. No cooking involved.

These are a few sample ideas. The one limitation is availability, but you can find most of these products in any good Asian market. Tom Douglas, a well-known chef and restaurant owner in Seattle (Etta's, Dahlia Lounge, Palace Kitchen), is always winning awards for his innovative seafood dishes. A humble fellow, he shrugs them off and gives credit to the Asian markets that he haunts for ideas. You can do that, too. If you live in Browning, Montana, and don't have an Asian market nearby, try the Internet.

Follow your fish. Be innovative. Your guests will love it.

# Eel Stewed in Red Wine

Eel must be purchased fresh, preferably live and skinned immediately. If you want to do this yourself, go ahead. Or, have the fishmonger do it for you on the day you plan to prepare the dish. Although very popular throughout Europe and in Asia, eel has not developed a huge following in North America.

### Serves 4

2 tablespoons butter

3 pounds fresh eel, cleaned, skinned, and cut into 1-inch pieces

1 cup sliced onions

2 cloves garlic, chopped

2 tablespoons flour

1 cup red wine

1 cup good-quality beef or veal stock

1 bay leaf

1 sprig thyme

$1/2$ teaspoon salt plus more to taste

Freshly ground black pepper

2 tablespoons chopped fresh parsley

In a large skillet with a lid, melt the butter over medium-high heat until it is foaming. Pat the eel dry and sear in the butter to a golden brown on all sides. Lift out the eel pieces and add the onions and garlic to the pan. Sauté the onions until they are tender and golden brown, 5 minutes. Dust the onions with the flour and cook for 1 minute more. Pour on the wine and the stock and stir to blend, using a wooden spoon to loosen any brown bits that may have stuck to the bottom of the pan. Return the eel to the pan and season with the bay leaf, thyme, $1/2$ teaspoon salt, and pepper to taste. Bring the liquid just to a boil, decrease the heat to a simmer, cover, and stew for 12 to 14 minutes. The eel will be tender and the sauce thick and shiny.

Discard the thyme and bay leaf and season the sauce with chopped parsley and additional salt and pepper as needed.

# Halibut Cheeks en Pappillote

Seafood alternatives: Salmon, Pacific Rockfish, Scallops, Snapper

Cooking seafood in parchment paper is a great way to seal in flavors without adding a lot of extra fat. It is also a simple and dramatic presentation for entertaining. Once you feel comfortable with the technique, try experimenting with your own favorite combination of vegetables and seasoning.

## Serves 4

4 tablespoons olive oil

2 pounds halibut cheeks

1 cup red onion, thinly sliced

1 small tomato, thinly sliced

4 sprigs fresh rosemary

4 sprigs fresh tarragon

4 cloves garlic, minced

1/4 teaspoon salt

1/4 teaspoon freshly ground black pepper

Juice of 1 lemon

Cut four 12 by 12-inch pieces of parchment paper. Rub each sheet with a 2 tablespoons of the olive oil and divide the halibut cheeks, onion, tomato, rosemary, tarragon, garlic, salt, and pepper evenly among the parchment pieces. Drizzle with the remaining olive oil and lemon juice.

Fold each piece of parchment to completely enclose the ingredients. Roll and pinch the paper to tightly seal. Place the packets on a baking sheet in the refrigerator until ready to bake.

Preheat oven to 350°.

Bake for 12 to 14 minutes, until the packet edges are just slightly brown and you can hear the juices sizzling inside.

Place one packet on each plate and cut into the top with kitchen shears for easy opening. Serve immediately.

# Cod Chowder:
# A Vainglorious Pursuit

MY HOME-PACK ARRIVED! A present from my son (the fisherman): a 40-pound case of cod from the Bering Sea. Luckily, I still have some stock left over from last year—the quintessence of 20 cod carcasses that I boiled in the backyard until the bark was falling off the trees. The result was a gallon jug of concentrated cod essence, potent enough to burn holes in the carpet. As the poet Yeats said, "You can't separate the dancer from the dance"—or the stock from the chowder. Without a good stock, you're dancing on one foot.

Of course, there are shortcuts. I know. I've tried them all. Clam nectar, for example. I've actually seen it recommended in some cod chowder recipes. But if you're going to use clam nectar, why not make *clam* chowder?

I'm talking *authentic* cod chowder here. Cod is an honest fish and deserves an honest chowder. But it's not easy. Roger Berkowitz of Legal Seafoods in Boston claims it was the stock that made the difference in his famous "inaugural" cod chowder, which was served at the inauguration of Ronald Reagan in 1981. I tasted it myself, truly superb. But what Berkowitz doesn't tell you is that he didn't use cod carcasses in it.

And I know the reason: because you need a mountain of them to extract one drop of cod flavor, which is why South Americans like their cod salted—and Norwegians douse them in lye, turning them into *lutefisk*—to give them some taste. Or that Berkowitz of all people (a Boston Codfather) should resort to monkfish and flounder frames to make his famous "cod" chowder.

People love cod because it's so mild, like a breath of ocean air. Toss a catfish into a boiling cauldron (experts say simmer, not boil, a fine point in my cookery), and your stock will be scratching in the kettle. Or a carp into the cauldron throw and you'll have to move out of your house. You've heard of Hemingway's "a moveable feast"? Carp is a moveable fish. The smell will follow you wherever you go. When you buy it in the store, it's kosher; but direct from the river it's an assault on the neighborhood when you cook it. But boil up a cod and all you'll smell after two or three hours is a whiff of the seashore.

Keep boiling. It takes faith to make a genuine cod chowder. And a little madness.

But what if you don't have any cod carcasses? In this case, you have two choices: Don't call it cod chowder, call it fish chowder—and put anything in it you want, including cod. Or you can pull a Berkowitz and call it a cod chowder, but use the carcasses from other fish to make the stock. It will be easier and, I confess, tastier to do so. The key to a good stock is using tasty fish, preferably bottomfish species such as sole, flounder, monkfish, sand dabs, rockfish, and so on—but no darker-fleshed species such as mackerel or tuna.

Black cod (a.k.a. sablefish) is ideal for a good stock. It's expensive, but you'll only need a little bit (frame or flesh) for all the flavor you need. In fact, if you just had the water the black cod swam through, that would do it. It's an extremely flavorful fish.

Add some celery and carrots to the stock. You'll strain them out along with what's left of the carcasses. Chef Rolin Henin, a former coach of the U.S. Culinary Olympic Team, taught me how to make my first stock. We came back from a fishing trip with some beautiful salmon—starving by the time we got to my house. I whacked off a couple of big salmon steaks ready to scorch them on the barbecue, but Henin insisted on making a sauce—and that, of course, meant making a stock.

Half water, half fish parts, some vegetables (as mentioned before; leeks and onions are also good), simmer for about an hour—that was how he did it. Next came the sauce, but I don't remember much about the sauce, only that we kept sprinkling wine into it and toasting the day's catch—*Magnifique! Magnifique!*—until the sauce tasted so good it was singing in the pan. Or we were singing. In any case, it was a success.

Making a stock isn't exactly what you'd call fast food, but it's well worth the effort. Almost any good seafood sauce (or chowder or soup) will start with a stock. All you really need are some fish trimmings, preferably fresh, and above all a nice fish head. A fish head will add authority to your stock. Shrimp heads will also work, providing a very nice (and robust) flavor.

The best fish stocks I've ever made didn't come from boiling cod carcasses in the backyard, but from the liquid leftover after poaching a fish. I strain it and then freeze it in ice-cube trays—to use it again next time. It just keeps getting better and better. The poaching liquid is, in itself, a wonderful sauce, perhaps perked up with a little splash of wine—but forget the cream. Smothering a nice piece of fish in a cream sauce is a culinary crime, in my opinion.

So, save all your fish heads. As my French fishing partner would say, *"Comment serait la vie sans une bonne sauce? Et la sauce sans un bon bouillon de base?"* What is life without a great sauce? And what is a great sauce without a great stock?

# Fish Stock

A good stock is the basis of all good soups, stews, and sauces. Creating a perfect fish stock is a slightly different technique than a hearty meat or chicken broth. Long slow simmering is unnecessary because all of the flavor can be released from the fish in about an hour. A very gentle simmer is required to keep the stock clear; fish carcasses (also known as frames) are best for clarity. Fish heads also make a very flavorful stock.

### Makes 3 quarts

2 pounds white fish frames, scraps, or fish heads

1 to 2 onions, quartered

2 cloves garlic

2 stalks celery, cut into 2-inch pieces

1 bulb fennel, thickly sliced

2 leeks, green part only, thickly sliced

2 bay leaves

4 parsley stems, bruised

1 lemon, quartered

2 cups white wine

2 or 3 sprigs thyme

8 to 10 black peppercorns

Place all of the ingredients in very large stockpot. Add cold water to cover the ingredients. Bring the liquid just to a boil. Immediately reduce the heat to a very gentle simmer and cook for 1 hour. Carefully lift out the largest pieces from the stock, and then strain the liquid through a fine sieve or cheesecloth. Chill until ready to use.

For a more concentrated stock, boil the stock and reduce by three-quarters. (Boil the stock only after it has been strained.) Freeze the concentrated stock in ice cube trays for convenience.

# Lobster or Shrimp Stock

Once you taste the nectar that is stock made from leftover shrimp or lobster shells, you will never discard them as trash again. Next time you find yourself peeling shrimp, save the shells in the freezer. When you have a good stash, spend an hour and make this colorful, flavorful stock for use in rich sauces, rice dishes, or bisques.

### Makes 6 to 8 cups

2 tablespoons olive oil

1 cup peeled and diced carrot

1 cup diced onion

1 cup sliced leek, green part only

3 cloves garlic

4 to 6 cups lobster or shrimp shells

2 tablespoons tomato paste

1/2 cup brandy

8 to 10 cups chicken stock or clear fish stock

1 or 2 sprigs fresh thyme, or 1/4 teaspoon dried thyme

3 to 4 parsley stems, bruised

8 to 10 black peppercorns

Heat the olive oil in a stockpot over medium heat. Cook the carrot, onion, leek, and garlic for 4 to 5 minutes until tender and aromatic. Add the shells and cook a few minutes more, until they are coated with the oil and vegetables and start to turn red. Add the tomato paste and stir to mix well. Cook 1 minute more. Pour on the brandy and reduce by half. Add the stock, thyme, parsley, and peppercorns.

Bring the stock to a boil, then decrease the heat to a gentle simmer. Cook for 1 hour. Strain through a fine sieve or cheesecloth and discard the shells and vegetables.

Keep the stock refrigerated or frozen until ready to use.

# Seafood Not So Simple

SEAFOOD IS PROOF that things are never quite what they seem. This was amply demonstrated to me on a recent trip to New England, where I expected to dine on franks and beans. Common knowledge was that New England's fisheries had collapsed, leaving an acute shortage of fish. Landings were at an all-time low.

What a surprise, then, to discover wonderful seafood everywhere I went! Not *any* seafood, mind you, but cod, haddock, and sole—the holy trinity of New England fish—and lobster, crabs, and scallops, all in abundance even as fishermen stayed ashore demonstrating for government assistance.

Could it be . . . *surimi?* Artificial cod masquerading as New England seafood?

Nonsense. Only God can make a cod or a haddock. And they were "on special" at almost every roadside restaurant in Massachusetts, Maine, and New Hampshire. I'd see a sign saying "Baked Haddock," and I couldn't help myself, fighting my way through the foliage freaks (it was October) to face yet another fillet of haddock. I ate so much haddock that I was beginning to develop a lateral stripe down my side. That's how you tell the difference between a cod and a haddock (they're close cousins, but the dark, lateral stripe is the giveaway). If I had to think of one good reason to move back to New England, it would be haddock.

In Portsmouth, New Hampshire, I switched to cod (baked in crumbs with butter and lemon). I poked it and probed it, but it was definitely mother's milk. The scrod was excellent as well. *Scrod* is a confusing term to most outsiders. What it means is baby cod, very succulent.

In New Bedford, I had scallops. New Bedford is famous for scallops, although the catch is a shadow of what it once was. For many years, New Bedford was the number one fishing port in the United States, but that honor now goes to Dutch Harbor, Alaska. As I say, the East Coast has fallen on hard times when it comes to fish. It can only get better, and in some cases it already has (as in the New Bedford scallop industry). On the other hand, the average weight of an East Coast swordfish these days is less than a hundred pounds (a 67-pound average is what I read). The babies are all that's left, making the stories of this solitary gladiator *(Xiphias gladius)* attacking whaling ships—and sinking them, too—seem more myth than reality.

A few notable exceptions to be sure, but all in all a sad story of badly depleted resources. So, where were all these fish coming from? Haddock out of no haddock, cod out of no cod . . . it didn't add up.

Call it Yankee ingenuity. The haddock was from Norway. The cod was from Alaska. The scallops were from China. The oysters were from Washington. And the swordfish was from Chile. At least the leaves on the trees were still from New England.

But here's a story within a story. How could this fish taste so fresh when it came from so far? Frozen at sea—a superior way to freeze fish because it locks in the quality while the fish are still very fresh. Even cod-conscious Yankees couldn't tell the difference.

And "fresh" takes a beating when fish get scarce. Fishermen have to stay out longer to make it pay, weeks on end sometimes. Someone should have said stop, this is crazy, but they didn't—or they did and weren't heard. When reason finally prevailed (the fisheries were severely curtailed), the damage was already done. Now, as I say, it's coming back, but slowly. It's funny how Nature can work against you. Fewer cod (because of overfishing) means more feed in the water. More feed in the water means more sharks and skates. More sharks and skates mean fewer baby cod—and around it goes.

Not that catastrophes are limited to New England. There are plenty to go around. The lesson is in how long it takes them to recover—if at all. Abalone in California. Yukon River chums. Bristol Bay "reds." The decline of wild salmon in the Pacific. Ask whose fault, and fists are flying.

And seafood consumers should get into the fray. After all, it's our fish: we the people. One side wants to feed it all to the sea lions, the other wants to catch every last fish. All I want is to eat a little of it—and to know that my dinner isn't contributing to the demise of a species, or that I'm the victim of antifishing propaganda.

Meanwhile, everything appears normal. New England still has its cod, even if it's from someplace else—and frozen at that. As one old codfather whispered to me: "I don't care where a fish is from or whether it's frozen or fresh, if the quality is there, I'll sell it."

He also wanted me to tell you that not all New England seafood is in short supply. Lobstah is abundant. Cod are being landed in limited quantities. Scallops are on the upswing. Maine is harvesting sea urchins now—for the Asian market. Cape shark (dogfish) is going strong—exported to Germany and England for fish and chips. And there's always the fall foliage.

So, don't worry about the franks and beans. The fish has never been better—or "fresher"—than it is today in the "Home of the Bean and the Cod."

# Smoked Black Cod Cakes

Seafood alternatives: Any Flaked Fish, Crab

Smoked black cod (sablefish) is an amazingly rich, succulent fish. The price has recently skyrocketed, so it is more economical to stretch the fish in this variation of a classic crab cake. Cold-smoked black cod is available through the Portlock Website and mail-order catalog.

## Serves 6

1¹/₂ pounds cold-smoked black cod

1 cup water

1 cup milk

3 eggs

¹/₂ red bell pepper, seeded and finely diced

1 stalk celery, finely diced

1¹/₂ tablespoons Dijon mustard

1 tablespoon chopped fresh garlic

4 dashes of Tabasco sauce

¹/₄ teaspoon salt (optional)

¹/₄ teaspoon freshly ground black pepper

3 tablespoons chopped fresh parsley

5 cups soft white bread crumbs

Oil for frying

Poach the cod by placing the pieces in an ovenproof dish with the water and milk. Bake for 20 to 25 minutes, until the top of the fish cracks. Let cool. Lift the cod from the poaching liquid and pat dry. Carefully remove and discard any skin and bones.

Flake the fish into a medium bowl. Add the eggs, bell pepper, celery, mustard, garlic, Tabasco sauce, salt, pepper, and half of the parsley. Stir in 1¹/₂ cups of the bread crumbs. Shape the mixture into ¹/₄-cup balls.

Mix together the remaining parsley and bread crumbs. Place a thin layer of this mixture in the bottom of a container. Place the fish balls on top, and cover with the remaining parsley and bread crumb mixture. Chill at least 30 minutes, or up to 2 days.

To cook the cakes, lift the balls from the loose bread crumbs and shape into discs. Heat a skillet over medium heat and fry the cod cakes in ¹/₄ inch of oil until they are golden brown on all sides, about 3 minutes.

If you are not serving the cod cakes immediately, brown them in the oil and then place them in a single layer on a cookie sheet. Chill or freeze. Reheat the cod cakes in a 350° oven for 30 minutes.

Serve warm.

# Lobster Risotto

Seafood alternatives: Jumbo Shrimp, Crawfish, Scallops

This is a rich and terribly decadent recipe, so serve it in small portions. Risotto makes an elegant variation to a soup or pasta course. It is also an economical way to serve lobster because a little goes a long way. For a treat, serve spoonfuls of warm, creamy risotto on a steamed artichoke bottom.

## Serves 4 to 6

One (1½-pound) live lobster, or two (8 to 10-ounce) frozen lobster tails, thawed

2 tablespoons olive oil

¼ cup finely minced shallot

½ cup minced leek, white part only

1½ cups arborio rice

½ cup white wine

5 cups lobster stock (see page 134)

2 to 3 tablespoons butter

To cook the live lobster, lunge it into a large pot of boiling water. When the water comes back to the boil, start timing the cooking. Cook the lobster for 5 minutes for each pound. (The lobster should be slightly undercooked for best results.) Drain and cool the lobster. Remove the meat from the shell and dice. Save the shells in the freezer for future batches of lobster stock.

(continued)

(continued from page 139)

**2 tablespoons freshly squeezed lemon juice**

**2 teaspoons chopped fresh tarragon**

**1/2 teaspoon salt**

**1/2 teaspoon freshly ground black pepper**

**1 tablespoon chopped fresh parsley**

**1 cup diced fresh tomato**

To make the risotto, heat the olive oil in a heavy-bottomed saucepan over medium heat. Gently cook the shallot and leek until they are completely tender, but not brown, 8 to 10 minutes. Stir in the rice and coat well with the oil and vegetables. Deglaze the pan with the white wine and bring to a gentle boil. Add the warm lobster stock 1/2 cup at a time, stirring well with a wooden spoon between each addition until the rice absorbs the liquid. Repeat until almost all of the stock is absorbed and the rice is tender, but not mushy, about 20 minutes.

Finally, add just enough of the remaining stock to loosen the rice slightly. Stir in the reserved lobster meat, butter, lemon juice, and tarragon. Season with salt and pepper.

Spoon the risotto onto small serving dishes and garnish with chopped parsley and diced tomato. Serve immediately.

# Romancing Raw Fish

 EVER THINK OF EATING RAW FISH? Maybe you'd rather have sashimi. It's the same thing, but it sounds a lot better. The word *sashimi,* has such a shimmering sound—Sa-SHEE-Mee—that we forget what it is. We taste it, we love it. But mostly we shun it. The main fear is that it will taste "fishy" (raw fish *never* tastes fishy, only bad fish tastes fishy) and that sushi bars, where most of us get our first taste of sashimi, are too formal to be comfortable. (Not true, unless eating fish with your fingers and giggling is what you'd call formal.)

Why Western culinary tradition is so devoid of raw fish, I can't say. We pickle it, marinate it, smoke it, salt it, but nowhere (that I can find) do we eat it raw. The closest match is an Eskimo dish called *tipnuk,* in which raw fish is buried in the tundra and exhumed months later when it's the consistency of cottage cheese—an acquired taste, to be sure.

Luckily, we have sushi bars where we can eat raw fish without digging it up. Sushi—raw fish with rice—has become as American as fried clams. At a sushi bar we can eat raw fish that is as exquisitely fresh as tipnuk is exquisitely rotten. But you don't have to go to a sushi bar to do it. You can eat raw fish right in your own igloo. Sashimi, in addition to being exquisitely fresh, is exquisitely *simple.* All you need is some very fresh fish (not more than four or five days old), soy sauce, Japanese horseradish *(wasabi),* and pickled ginger (to clear the palate).

As with any raw food, some common sense is in order. I suggest you start with raw tuna—yellowfin (*ahi,* as it's often called), bluefin, or bigeye. Tuna is problem-free and available year-round. Japan's infatuation with sashimi began with tuna—and so very likely will yours.

No two tunas are alike. The way tuna is graded is by color, fat content, and freshness. Prime specimens (large bluefin, for example) will bring up to $50,000 for a single fish on Tokyo's Tsukiji Market. Don't worry, you can get by much cheaper.

*Maguro* is the most common cut of tuna, almost always yellowfin, but sometimes bigeye. The flesh should be ruby-red, slightly translucent, absolutely odorless, and should melt in your mouth like candy.

*Toro* is another cut of tuna, richer and fattier than maguro, a favorite of connoisseurs.

My favorite sashimi isn't tuna at all, but yellowtail *(hamachi),* a species that is farmed in Japan. I highly recommend it. The flesh isn't reddish, as it is with tuna, but more of an ivory color. Don't be thrown off by the name *yellowtail.* There are a lot of fish called yellowtail that aren't hamachi; their close relative off California and Mexico *(Seriola dorsalis)* is a very different culinary experience: leaner, darker, and much stronger tasting.

Beyond these, almost any finfish species that's fresh enough will make passable, if not excellent, sashimi. *Avoid freshwater species, however, unless previously frozen, including wild salmon.* Farmed salmon are okay. The idea here is not to expose yourself to any unpleasant organisms that would normally be killed during cooking. Freshwater species will sometimes ingest tapeworm larvae. More you do not want to know.

One more thing. If you're in Hawaii or some other exotic place and, like me, you're a do-it-yourself sashimi buff, make some inquiries before you eat any reef species, especially if you're spearing or catching them yourself. There's a very dangerous toxin called ciguaterra that's found in reef species in certain areas. It has to do with a tiny organism that's associated with a certain kind of algae. The fish eats the algae and you eat the fish (or eat another fish that ate the fish that ate the algae), and you'll need more than Doctor Seuss to make you better. Depending on the year, Hawaii loses more people to ciguaterra than it does to sharks.

That's it on the scary stuff.

As always, buy with your eyes. In the case of tuna, look for good flesh color (red to deep-red, but not brown), brightness, and a slight translucency (raw tuna should never be completely opaque, a sign of mishandling). Always ask your dealer for "sashimi-grade" tuna.

One more thing. Never have sashimi pre-sliced. Do it yourself just before serving to preserve color and freshness. Do as the Japanese: "Eat with your eyes."

Is it sushi or sashimi? This always confuses people. Sushi literally means "vinegared rice." In a sushi bar, it's finger-rolls of rice with strips of sashimi hand-pressed into them or into any number of other rolls, such as the California Roll, Tuna Roll, Cucumber Roll, and so on.

Finger-rolls are a snap; the main thing is getting the rice right (sticky, but not mushy). The popular California Roll is very simple—avocado, cucumber, and crab or shrimp rolled in rice. But traditional sushi rolls can be challenging, containing as many as six items, usually wrapped in dried seaweed *(nori)*.

Don't let tradition stand in your way. Roll your own. If you have rockfish, call it Rock & Roll; if it's eel *(onaga)*, call it The Love Roll. Whatever you want. (I hate somber sushi.)

There are dozens of how-to books on sushi, but there's no substitute for a trip to your local sushi bar, where you can see all the tricks of the trade firsthand.

Let's do some sushi. The place I have in mind is Matsuhisa's, a small, venerable sushi bar located in Beverly Hills. (You didn't think I'd take you to a dump, did you?) The smell of jasmine fills our nostrils as we enter the room. Robert DeNiro, Gene Hackman, George Segal, Madonna are all regulars—or were when I hung out here. Once, I sat next to George Segal, who was very entertaining—and a great lover of sushi. The glass showcase along the bar glistens with fish: octopus *(tako)*, shrimp *(ebi)*, sea urchin roe *(uni)*, eel *(onago)*, salmon *(sake)*, and so forth.

Let's start with some sea urchin roe (gonads actually) followed by octopus tentacle. Already, I can see tears streaming down your face. At last, you're eating with your eyes! Or is it the wasabi? Surely not the octopus tentacle? The little suction cups are perfectly harmless, kind of ticklish when they stick to your tongue. And the creamy sea urchin roe, so wonderful. I know you're going to love it!

But it might take a little while to get used to, very natural. I'll just leave you here with the rest of the celebrities to experiment . . . because that's what you do in a sushi bar, sample this, sample that. You won't like everything, but don't worry. The ocean is full of raw fish.

# Seared Herb-Crusted Tuna with Radish Salad and Wasabi Mayonnaise

Seafood alternatives: Sashimi-Grade Albacore Tuna

Seared tuna is served virtually raw, so it is important to select only the highest grade, sashimi tuna and use it the day you buy it. The fish is just briefly cooked in a hot pan and the rich, firm meat stands up well to the peppery herb blend. Note that the tuna is in small portions, because a little fish goes a long way. If you have even a small patch of garden, this may soon become a favorite recipe for you to showcase your harvest. Seasoned rice vinegar and powdered wasabi (Japanese green horseradish) are available at many supermarkets and specialty food stores.

| Serves 4 |
| --- |

### Radish Salad

1 cup quartered and sliced red radishes (¹/₂ bunch)

1 cup quartered and sliced English cucumber (¹/₂ cucumber)

2 tablespoons chopped red onion

2 green onions, sliced

¹/₄ cup seasoned rice vinegar

¹/₄ teaspoon salt

Freshly ground black pepper

Prepare the Radish Salad first. Toss together all of the ingredients in a bowl. Set aside while you prepare the fish.

On a plate or shallow dish, mix together the chopped parsley, oregano, rosemary, thyme, shallot, garlic, salt, and pepper. Evenly coat the fish with the herb mixture.

(continued)

(continued from page 145)

3 tablespoons chopped fresh parsley

1 tablespoon chopped fresh oregano

1 teaspoon chopped fresh rosemary

1 tablespoon chopped fresh thyme

1 shallot, minced

1 clove garlic, minced

$1/2$ teaspoon salt

1 teaspoon freshly ground black pepper

Four (4-ounce) sashimi-grade tuna steaks

2 tablespoons olive oil

8 crisp baby romaine lettuce leaves

$1/2$ cup mayonnaise mixed with 1 teaspoon prepared wasabi

Heat the olive oil in a large skillet over high heat. When the oil just barely starts to smoke, place 2 tuna steaks in the pan and sear for about 1 minute, until the tuna is lightly brown. Flip the fish and cook another minute. Remove the steaks from the pan and wipe the pan to remove any bits that may burn between batches. Repeat with the remaining pieces of fish.

To serve, place 2 lettuce leaves on each plate. Slice a tuna steak and fan over the lettuce. Top with a generous spoonful of Radish Salad and drizzle with the wasabi mayonnaise. Serve immediately.

# Chirashi Sushi (Scattered Sushi)

Scattered sushi is one of the most spectacular dishes served at traditional Japanese restaurants. A bowl is filled with seasoned sushi rice and topped with fresh, glistening seafood. Because there is no rolling or shaping of the rice, it is very quick and easy as well as beautiful. Another appeal of chirashi sushi is that you can customize the dish to include a mixture of raw and cooked favorites or an assortment of fresh, blanched vegetables to appeal to most any palate.

### Serves 2

1 recipe sushi rice
(see page 148)

1 cooked lobster, or 4 medium shrimp, cooked and peeled

2 ounces raw sashimi-grade tuna, sliced

2 ounces tako (octopus), sliced

1 ounce raw geoduck, or
2 cooked surf clams

1 ounce raw scallop, thinly sliced

2 tablespoons tobiko caviar
(flying fish roe)

$1/2$ cup radish or pea sprouts

2 tablespoons pickled ginger

Prepared wasabi

Soy sauce

Fill two pretty bowls with sushi rice. Divide and arrange the remaining ingredients attractively on the rice. Serve with wasabi and soy sauce.

# Sushi Rice

### Makes 4 cups

2 cups California or Japanese
short grain rice

2 1/3 cups water

One 2 to 3-inch piece kombu
seaweed (optional)

### Seasoned rice vinegar

1/4 cup rice vinegar

2 tablespoons sugar

1 tablespoon mirin

1 tablespoon sake

1 1/2 teaspoons salt

Wash the rice in cool water until the rinse water runs clear and the rice is pearly. Drain and combine the rice and the measured water in a rice cooker or medium saucepan. Let the rice and water soak for at least 15 minutes.

To cook the rice in a saucepan, bring rice and water to a rolling boil. Stir and reduce heat to low. Add the kombu and cover the saucepan with a tight-fitting lid. Simmer for 15 minutes. Remove from heat. Let the rice stand, covered and undisturbed for another 15 minutes. Or cook according to the manufacturer's suggestion in an electric rice cooker.

Meanwhile, prepare the seasoned rice vinegar by stirring all of the ingredients together in a small bowl.

To make the sushi rice, move the cooked rice to a large, shallow bowl. Sprinkle the rice with some of the seasoned vinegar and gently mix into the rice with a wooden spoon. Continue as the rice absorbs the vinegar. While you are mixing the vinegar into the rice a little at a time, fan the steam away to cool the rice. Each grain of rice should be lightly coated with the vinegar and shiny, but not soaked or mushy.

If you are not using the rice immediately, cover with a damp towel and keep at room temperature for up to 6 hours. Do not refrigerate or the rice becomes hard.

# Dining with Sea Lion Murphy

I GOT A LETTER THE OTHER DAY from the museum in Valdez, Alaska, informing me that my old boat, the *Perry*, had been inducted into their maritime collection: "a part of Alaska's small-boat history," wrote the curator. This got me to thinking about my old friend Sea Lion Murphy. If anyone taught me the secrets of seafood (more than I wanted to know) it was Joe Kompkoff.

Kompkoff was his surname, but everyone knew him as Sea Lion Murphy, so dubbed in Murphy's Bar in Cordova, circa 1975, when he came in and ordered a steak, flipped out at the bill—fourteen dollars!—swearing that he used to feed an entire village for fourteen cents: the cost of one cartridge to kill a sea lion.

Sea Lion wasn't listed among the former owners of the *Perry*, a list going back to 1934, the year she was built on Perry Island in Prince William Sound, but he probably caught more fish on her than anyone. I teamed up with him in 1979, the year I bought the *Perry* for five hundred dollars down. She was my stake in the smaller scheme of things; Sea Lion was hired as my skipper and our two sons, both 12, were the crew.

Sea Lion had a lot of trouble on shore—with drink and with wives—but on the water he was still an Aleut chief: "the Fox of Prince William Sound," as he was known by other fishermen. He had a lot of names, not all of them good. He was short, powerfully built, with closely cropped gray hair and deep, vertical scars on his face where he had been clawed by a bear cub.

The bear cub was his pet. One day he was walking with it when some dogs attacked. The cub panicked and climbed the nearest "tree," which happened to be him. He finally gave it away, but not before it shredded all the furniture in his house, and his wife, I forget which one, left him.

Sea Lion was part of an Aleut community that had been evacuated from the Aleutian Islands during World War II, when the Japanese started attacking the islands (a little-known fact of history). I've seen the bullet holes myself in the old hospital in Unalaska. After the war, the government never relocated the families, leaving them scattered across the state. To an outsider, an Aleut looks like any other native, but to them, living in places like Cordova or Ketchikan was like being a stranger in a strange land.

The Aleuts have always been a breed apart—very tied to their land, which they defended with a fury. I remember reading about them as a kid. The men were said to have slept with one eye open, a club in one hand to defend their village against attackers. They were fierce fighters and great fishermen, traveling across the Bering Sea in their seal-skin kayaks, fishing, and hunting seals to support their villages through the winter.

At first, it was hard to connect any of these qualities to my friend. He was a lost soul, an Aleut hunter reduced to washing dishes in the local bars. It wasn't that he couldn't change, he didn't want to change. I remember sitting in his tiny room in the Alaska Hotel in Cordova, trying to explain to him what child support was all about. He had just received a letter from the State of Alaska.

But aboard the *Perry*, as I say, he was still an Aleut hunter. His rifle was never out of reach, and he shot his share of seals that summer we fished together (legal under Alaska's "subsistence" law). The only problem was that we had to eat them. Seal has the taste of cod liver oil multiplied a thousand times. Once you got it down, the worst was yet to come, building up in your bowels to explosive force. Sea Lion kept a big jar of anti-gas pills in the foc'sle or we probably would have died of asphyxiation.

He clung to the old ways even though it cost him dearly. Like the time he shot a baby seal, and while he was cleaning it on deck, he heard a loud clattering coming from the stern. His wife was throwing all the pots and pans over the side in protest—whether out of sympathy for the seal or the prospect of having to eat it, I don't know.

That summer, we fished with the Aleut "fleet," a rag-tag group of boats that tied up together at the end of the day, traded fish stories, and shared dinner. Dinner is what we dreaded the most. Every night it was on a different boat. Sometimes we were invited, sometimes not—and we prayed hard to be spared the honor.

You cannot imagine what it's like to sit in a circle of Aleuts sharing a seal for dinner—excellent company, mind you, except for the seal. Even the Aleuts didn't like it. Boats were forever pulling up alongside us. "Hey, Joe, we got a nice baby seal for you." "No thanks, we already have two. Do you know anyone who needs one?"

It was served sliced in small pieces with whole raw onions on the side to dampen the taste. One small bite of seal, one big bite of onion, tears streaming down our faces.

Such was the power of their culture that they kept on eating it.

Mostly we ate salmon. Sea Lion would pick it out from our catch that day, usually a sockeye, his favorite, and invariably would poach it. For years after, I prepared almost every fish I ate poached, tossing fresh vegetables into the poacher with it, saving the liquid for another time when it would taste even better.

To Sea Lion, no part of the fish was the same, preferring the bellies because they had the most fat and therefore the most flavor. The "squaw candy" that you see in some parts of Alaska (hard-smoked strips of salmon) are made from bellies. And, of course, the belly is the richest in omega-3, the miracle substance found almost exclusively in seafood—discovered, by the way, when Eskimos in eastern Canada were found to have almost no incidence of heart disease. Their diet was almost exclusively fish—and seal meat.

Of course, we didn't have fresh vegetables, or even rice (hard to do on a boat), but Sea Lion always had a surprise. One time he cooked up some salmon milt, the white, custardlike substance found in spawning males—in short, the sperm. "Now, we will catch some fish!" he'd exclaim, his scarred face crinkling in laughter, as we watched him slice it into slabs and put it on our plates. Now, drink your milt!

Tasteless stuff, but years later I read an article in a newspaper about a "medical breakthrough," a substance called protamine, which was used in heart surgery—extracted from salmon milt.

Salmon roe, on the other hand, was a delicacy—better than beluga caviar, and we ate it all the time, stripped from the skein on crackers with cream cheese or by itself. The best of it—called *ikura* by the Japanese—is from the chum salmon, but it must be eaten fresh (or fresh-frozen), not cured in a jar. Candy on a cracker, but so potent that I felt like running upstream every time we passed a river.

When we fished, we fished hard. The *Perry* was a small seiner. The way we caught salmon was to spot a school of fish, then encircle it with the purse seine, slowly pursing it back to the boat. When the net came alongside, thrashing with fish we hoped, we'd brail the salmon out of it with a smaller (hydraulically operated) scoop net.

We were a simple operation, to say the least. Other boats that we were competing with (not Aleut boats) had radar and sonar worth more than our boat. And some had spotter planes hired to scan the area for any signs of fish, radioing them in code to give them the location. Sockeye salmon was the quarry, a big money fish that year.

We didn't have a plane, but we had "the Fox." No one was catching anything, the spotter planes weren't finding any fish, and the radio was filled with angry talk about foreign fishermen intercepting all the salmon, and so on. Days went by like this.

Then, one evening, we got the signal from Sea Lion that he spotted a school. Boats were all around us looking for fish, so we had to play it cool or they'd push a small boat like us out of the way. We could tell Sea Lion was excited because he was spitting furiously. He always spit when he saw fish, and he was spitting like he was on the pitcher's mound in a World Series.

"Pull the pin!"

We let go the net, circling the school in a perfect set, the rest of the fleet stunned. We brailed well into the night, other boats coming over to watch us, unbelieving. I made enough money that night for a down payment on a house. Got my son in school and got a job working for a seafood magazine.

I have a lot of good memories of Sea Lion. His passion for fishing—and for all the natural things around him, like the little birds he used to rob out of their nests, their peeping piercing the air as he climbed the tree, the three of us holding our ears.

But I especially remember Sea Lion's sense of humor. "What are we having for dinner?" we'd ask at the end of a day's fishing. His answer was always the same— "Jellyfish sandwiches"—and we'd have a good laugh. Years later, at an exclusive Chinese restaurant in Los Angeles where I was interviewing a well-known radio host (a "raconteur" and "gourmet" as he described himself on his business card), I saw "Jellyfish Salad" on the menu. I had to smile. And I had to order it in honor of my old friend. It arrived jiggling on the plate.

# Seafood Pasta with Caviar

Seafood alternatives: Mussels, Squid, Rock Shrimp

Serve almost anyone a creamy dish of seafood and pasta and they will swoon. Add a dollop of caviar and you will have friends for life. You may substitute clam nectar or fish stock for the cream for a leaner variation.

## Serves 6

2 tablespoons olive oil

$1/4$ cup minced onion

3 cloves garlic, minced

$1/4$ teaspoon crushed red chile flakes

$1/2$ pound scallops

12 medium shrimp, peeled and deveined

1 pound clams, well scrubbed

$1/2$ cup dry white wine

1 cup heavy cream

2 tablespoons butter

$1/4$ teaspoon salt

Freshly ground black pepper

1 pound dry linguine

1 tablespoon chopped fresh parsley

2 to 4 ounces salmon caviar

Bring a large pot of salted water to a boil.

Heat the olive oil in a large skillet over medium heat and sauté the onion, garlic, and chile flakes until the onion is tender but not brown, about 3 minutes. Increase the heat to medium high and add the scallops and shrimp. Sear until the seafood is aromatic, but not cooked through, about 1 minute. Lift out the scallops and shrimp and set aside. Add the clams. Pour on the wine and reduce the liquid by half. Add the cream and simmer until the clams open and the sauce has reduced slightly, about 6 minutes more. Discard any clams that remain tightly closed. Return the scallops and shrimp to the sauce, whisk in the butter, and season with salt and pepper

Meanwhile, cook the pasta according to the package directions. Drain well and return to the empty pot. Toss the pasta with the seafood sauce and parsley. Cook over low heat for 1 minute until the pasta absorbs some of the sauce. Divide the pasta into warm serving bowls and top with a dollop of caviar. Serve immediately.

# Mudcrab Madness

"TWO MORE BUNDIES, PLEASE!"

Bundaberg Rum, that is. Dark stuff that makes you act like a pirate. Lee Marvin used to drink them (at the Cairns Sport Fishing Club, Cairns, Australia) with his Aussie skipper until they both got so tipsy they'd topple to the floor—or fall to it in a flurry of fists, depending on how well the fishing went that day. In the morning, they'd go back out to the marlin grounds the best of friends.

So we were told by the waitress. Marvin's legend is so vivid in these parts that I half-expected to see him mounted on the wall with the other trophies. Not that there's any shortage of characters here. In fact, I was supposed to go fishing with one, Marvin's former skipper, but the wind was up, and even the waters inside the Reef—Cairns being the nearest port to those fabled rocks, the Great Barrier Reef—were whipped into a froth.

Meanwhile, Johnny Mudcrab was telling me stories . . . about the time he parachuted mudcrabs out of a World War II Neptune bomber. He was targeting a beach in Queensland, where the crabs were to perform in a charity race. Each crab was fitted with a parachute. Even so, some of them broke their legs landing, but the Mudcrab Magician always had a few extra crab up his sleeve.

I was in Cairns at the end of a three-week tour of Australia's fishing industry under the auspices of AUSTRADE (Australia's trade promotion board). Cairns was my reward for behaving myself, a chance to consort with the natives and do some fishing.

But, excuse me, the Mudcrab Magician is off on another story. A crab race in Oklahoma City. He hired some cattle auctioneers to auction off the crabs. Fifty volunteers were on television taking bets on the race, all the money going to Christian charities. (Johnny is a born-again crustacean.)

"Why do you do this?" I asked him.

"Why, to dress up as a crab, mate," he says, sipping his Bundie. He showed me some pictures. Sure enough, there he was in a rubber suit with antennas protruding from his head and two giant rubber claws. "I have a sideways walk to make me look more realistic," he says, standing up and shuffling sideways around the floor, his hands snapping at the air like pincers.

Life on the crab racing circuit isn't easy, though. Keeping the crabs alive is the biggest problem, leading to all kinds of complications. Like the time he was kicked out of the Royal Hawaiian Hotel on Oahu (on the afternoon of a big race, no less) when the maid discovered crabs crawling around in the bathtub.

Emma, Johnny's daughter, joined us. She runs Johnny's mudcrab operation in Cairns, exporting live mudcrab around the world, as well as supplying local restaurants, where mudcrab is highly favored by Japanese tourists. This gives the Mudcrab Magician more time for his eccentricities, which, at the age of 57, are in full flower.

*"Another round of Bundies, say I, and damned be to the weather!"*

We ordered steamed mudcrab (Johnny having left a monster in the kitchen earlier, at least two kilos), some banana prawns, Morton Bay bugs, yabbies, a dozen Sydney rock oysters, and a whole grilled barramundi. Marvin came here to catch fish, I came here to eat them.

Australia's wealth of characters is exceeded only by its wealth of seafood. In the United States we just see lobster tails and orange roughy, a rather bland and expensive fish. Most of Australia's seafood goes to Asia.

And, of course, they eat a lot of it themselves. The Aussies have great seafood—and are great seafood eaters, much more sophisticated than you might think (I mean, the stereotype is lamb and alligators, right?). For example, an Aussie would never think of eating scallops, of which they have an abundance, without the roe intact. We don't even see the roe ("coral," as it's called here) and don't even know what it is! It's bright orange, lovely to look at, bland in taste, with a very pleasant texture—a definite bonus to the simple scallop. Why don't we see it on our scallops? Talk to the FDA. Most of our scallops are imported, and the coral is a problem for the FDA.

Or take the shrimp. At the Sydney Fish Market, said to be the largest retail fish market in the world, the stalls are overflowing with shrimp of every description—giant banana prawns, kings, and wild tigers—and all of them sold with heads-on. The heads, of course, carry the flavor, wonderful for reduction sauces or just to suck on, plus whole shrimp are beautiful to look at. So, why do we decapitate them?

The answer is that shrimp spoil much faster with heads-on, and shrimp boats fishing in the Gulf of Mexico (the source of almost all our domestic wild shrimp) fish for quantity, not quality, extending their trips to the maximum the shrimp will bear—and beyond. (That unique "iodine" taste that we associate with wild shrimp in this country doesn't exist in Australia. I'll say no more.) Plus, almost all the shrimp we consume in the United States is farmed anyway, and you wouldn't want to suck on the heads of farmed shrimp if you knew anything about high-density shrimp culture.

Great eaters, these Aussies, and great talkers. The problem is understanding them. The accent isn't that bad, but the vocabulary is odd, to say the least. If you hear an Aussie talk about eating "bugs," he means lobster. A girl is a "sheelah"; a nosy person is a "sickybeak"; a close look is a "Captain Cook"; the real thing is "fair dinkum" (or "dinky-di"); and writers' cramp is called "kangaroo's paw."

*"She was a fair dinkum sheelah, but her jackeroo was no poofter, giving me the Captain Cook like I was some blow-in ragbag."*

At last, our dinner arrived! The pièce de résistance was the mudcrab. We broke shell together, devouring the sweet, succulent flesh while Johnny regaled us with stories of the mudcrab's great strength: *"break a bloody beer bottle, that one . . ."*

The prawns arrived, and we began suckin' heads and pinchin' tails . . . *fair dinkum!*

But the best was the mudcrab. Don't be thrown off by the humble name. This crab is a famous delicacy throughout Australasia. It's harvested as far east as Samoa and Fiji and west into the Indian Ocean and across to the east coast of Africa. Or I should say overharvested. The species is in trouble because people like to eat them so much, but here's the good news. Farms are already gearing up for production in Australia, India, and the Philippines. No one thought it would happen with salmon or shrimp and it did—and will again with mudcrab. Why? Because the price is right.

Here's the way the chef in Cairns prepared our mudcrab: 1 teaspoon of garlic, 1 teaspoon of ginger, a glass of wine, a sprinkle of sugar, and a tad of cornstarch. The crab is cleaned (back removed), cut into four equal pieces, and put in the frying pan with a little bit of oil. (A good trick is to snip the tips off the ends of the claws and crack the legs so the liquid can permeate the crab as you cook it.) Add the garlic, ginger, and water to cover. Cook until the crab starts to turn red. Add the wine and simmer for about 6 minutes. A sprinkle of sugar and a little cornstarch for thickener, and you're ready to eat.

That's it. You can practice on a Dungeness crab while you're waiting for the mudcrab to arrive. If you can't wait, you can order mudcrab over the Internet from Queensland. The season is between December and May.

The next morning the sun came through my window blinds in a bunderburst of pain. Wincing, I got up and gave the water a Captain Cook. No fishing again today! No problem. There's more than one fish to fry in Cairns. You can fry your body on the beach, for one thing. Or you can take one of the many cruises in the bay, where the wind will straighten your hair, but it's still a lot calmer than the Great Barrier.

I decided to go mud-crabbing. You catch the crab, they cook it for you. I met the boat at the dock along with six other tourists, all Japanese. We bowed to one another and stepped aboard. To each his own madness.

# Grilled Lobster with Toasted Almond Butter

This is a superb way to serve lobster. The smoky flavors from the grill and garlicky nut butter really bring out the sweetness of the meat. You may start indulging in lobster more often. This is a perfect celebration dish for anniversaries, graduations, or even long weekends. If you want to cook only two lobsters, make the same amount of butter, but freeze the leftovers for your next fish fillet.

### Serves 4

¹/₄ cup whole blanched almonds

2 cloves garlic, minced or pressed

¹/₄ cup chilled butter, cut into cubes

1 tablespoon chopped fresh parsley

Salt

Freshly ground black pepper

4 live Maine or Australian lobsters (about 1¹/₂ pounds each)

Preheat the oven to 350°.

Toast the almonds on a baking sheet until well browned, 12 to 13 minutes. Let cool.

Finely chop the cooled almonds in a food processor. Add the garlic and pulse a few times more. Add the butter and blend until well combined. Mix in the parsley with salt and pepper to taste. Scrape the almond butter into a bowl and set aside.

Preheat an outdoor grill.

Bring a large pot of water to a rolling boil. Add the lobsters and boil for 5 minutes, cooking them in batches if necessary. Drain well and rinse in cold water. Split the lobsters lengthwise with a large, sharp knife. Remove the viscera from the lobster bodies and gently crack the claws (leaving them intact). Brush the exposed meat of each split tail with about 1 teaspoon of the almond butter.

Place the split lobsters, buttered-side down, on the preheated grill and cook for 2 minutes. Turn the lobsters over and brush generously with additional butter. Grill for 2 minutes longer. Remove the lobsters from the grill and press some of the almond butter into the cracked claws. Serve immediately.

# Big Shrimp

Everyone loves Big Shrimp! But what is the best way to cook them to justify the price? On the *barbie,* of course. First, inspect shrimp closely before you buy. Avoid any with black spots or discoloration. Don't waste your money if they are at all mushy or strong smelling. There should be no aroma of ammonia. If you are lucky enough to find fresh shrimp that still have bright, clear heads, you know they are fresh. Cooking the shrimp in their shells adds immensely to the flavor and color. Two or three really big shrimp are enough for most people.

### Serves 4

1/2 cup (4 ounces) butter

2 cloves garlic, pressed or minced

1 tablespoon freshly squeezed lemon juice

Dash of Worcestershire sauce

Freshly ground black pepper

1 tablespoon freshly chopped mixed herbs (such as thyme, basil, or parsley)

1 1/2 pounds of big shrimp, in the shell

Preheat an outdoor grill.

Melt the butter. Stir in the garlic, lemon, Worcestershire sauce, and pepper. Remove from the heat and add the herbs. Keep warm while you grill the shrimp.

Place the shrimp on the grill. Close the lid and grill for 2 minutes. Flip the shrimp, baste lightly with the herbed butter, close the lid, and continue to cook until the shrimp are lightly charred and cooked through, another 3 minutes.

Place the shrimp on a serving dish and spoon some of the herbed butter over. Serve immediately with the remaining butter alongside for dipping.

# A Fish Fallacy

 HERE'S A SEAFOOD QUIZ FOR YOU. Which is superior: seafood from warm water or from cold water? From the tropics or from the frigid waters of the North?

Normally, folks answer this question according to where they're from: New Englanders trust in cod—and wouldn't eat a corvina even if they knew what one was. Latin Americans, on the other hand, don't trust in cod, known to them as *bacalao,* a euphemism for shark. They'd rather eat corvina, the "cod" of Latin America. As one who has savored both, I can say they are equally wonderful.

Of course, I'm generalizing here. In Brazil they know very well what cod is, and they love it. But the point remains: too often we let our seafood ethnocentrism limit our choices—for example, the mistaken notion that coldwater species are somehow more robust (more firm-fleshed) than warmwater species, which I heard a Boston restauranteur refer to as "fluff fish."

Where does such an idea come from? Do people believe coldwater fish are partially frozen when they come out of the water—thus *firmer?* That warmwater fish have a looser lifestyle—drinking margaritas and sunbathing on the beach, ready to fall apart on your plate?

Species, not geography, dictates the texture (and taste) of a fish. Other factors enter into it: what the fish has been feeding on, whether it's spawning, how it was handled on the boat (left out in the sun or put in the fish-hold and iced immediately). Colder waters don't necessarily have anything to do with the quality of a fish. Some of the mushiest, softest-fleshed species in the ocean are from Arctic and Antarctic waters: the family of hakes, for example. Alaska pollock (a member of the cod family) is an example of a soft fish. Arrowtooth flounder, of the Bering Sea, fall apart on your fork. Pink salmon, the most abundant salmon in Alaska, are a mushy fish.

On the other hand, think of all the firm-fleshed fish from the tropics that are available at your local fish counter: groupers, snappers, tunas, marlins, mahimahi, shark. Warmwater lobster tails (from the Caribbean) sell at a discount compared to cold-water tails (Australia, New Zealand, South Africa) because the flesh is tougher, that is, firmer than lobster from colder waters.

But doesn't warmwater seafood *spoil* quicker?

I've heard that one a hundred times. In fact, the opposite is more the case. What causes spoiling after a fish comes out of the water is the *difference* between water temperature and air temperature: The greater the difference the more rapid the spoilage. And that difference is far less in most tropical countries than it is, say, in Alaska or New England.

The point I'm driving home here is that there is no *intrinsic* difference between warmwater and coldwater species. The difference comes in the handling of the fish. And here, it has to be admitted, there frequently is a difference. Any fish that is not iced immediately when it comes out of the water is heading for trouble. If it is left on deck under the sun, in temperatures approaching 80 degrees, it's really heading for trouble. To add coal to the fire, if it's a scombroid species—any dark-fleshed fish such as tuna, mahimahi, mackerel, or any of the jacks—it is a strong candidate for scombroid poisoning, a nonfatal but very serious gastric disorder resulting from the rapid build-up of histamines in the fish's flesh.

Thus, it goes without saying that seafood buyers should be particularly careful when they buy any scombroid species (firm flesh, good natural color, no bad smells). I've read that fish so contaminated have a peppery taste. I've also read that this is not true. Your eyes and nose are always your best warning system. (If it tastes peppery it's probably too late, anyway.)

What happens is the fish often gets the blame instead of the culprits who handle it. Ice is not always readily available, especially in developing countries, the result being that the seafood gets a bad name and the seafood buyer gets a bad stomachache. But here's good news. The Food & Drug Administration's new seafood safety policy, the so-called HACCP regulations, covers the sanitary conditions of any fish plant exporting to the United States, including refrigeration. The bad news is that these regulations aren't being enforced as strictly as they should.

Getting back to warmwater fallacies, another one is the notion that all seafood from "south of the border" is from warm water. What country do you associate with salmon, rainbow trout, oysters, lobster, king crab, and penguins? Chile, a South American country.

To make waters even murkier, some of our favorite fish (called pelagics) are neither warmwater nor coldwater, but both—summering off New England and Canada and wintering in the subtropics, as in the case of the Atlantic swordfish and bluefin tuna. And there's bluefish, a favorite summer species off New York and New Jersey that, like many of the residents of those states, winters in Florida.

As to which is superior, warmwater or coldwater species, the answer should be clear by now. Both. If the fish isn't what it should be, don't blame the fish. Otherwise, it all comes down to personal taste. Some say corvina, some say cod. My favorite fish is mahimahi . . . or is it haddock? It all depends on what's on my plate—and how well it's been handled.

# Snapper Vera Cruz Tacos

Seafood alternatives: Any Thick, Firm Whitefish; Mahimahi; Shrimp

Seafood tacos are always a popular dish for entertaining or for a healthy family dinner. These are made with a nod to the classic Huachinago Vera Cruz—snapper simmered in diced tomatoes and citrus. This recipe is relatively mild, but if you are a pepper-lover, it is a great one to really spice up. Substitute a habanero for the jalapeño, or splash in your favorite flame-throwing pepper sauce.

### Serves 4 to 6

2 tablespoons olive oil

1 cup chopped onion

4 cloves garlic, minced

1 jalapeño pepper, seeded and diced

1 serrano pepper, seeded and diced (optional)

2 cups diced tomato

$1/2$ cup freshly squeezed orange juice

2 tablespoons freshly squeezed lime juice

2 tablespoons tequila

1 teaspoon salt plus more to taste

$1/2$ teaspoon freshly ground black pepper plus more to taste

Heat the oil in a large skillet over medium heat. Add the onion, garlic, and peppers. Cook until tender and aromatic, 4 to 5 minutes. Add the tomato and cook another minute. Stir in the orange and lime juices, tequila, 1 teaspoon salt, and $1/2$ teaspoon pepper. Nestle the snapper fillets into the sauce, spooning the sauce over to cover. Bring the mixture to a gentle boil. Decrease the heat to medium and simmer until the fish fillets are just opaque through, 8 to 10 minutes.

1 1/2 pounds boneless, skinless red snapper fillet

1 tablespoon chopped fresh cilantro for garnish

12 corn tortillas

1 avocado, diced

2 oranges, segmented

4 cups lettuce or cabbage sliced thinly

2 green onions, green and white parts, thinly sliced

Hot sauce or salsa (optional)

Lift the fish from the sauce and arrange on a serving dish. Reduce the sauce slightly if necessary so the liquids cling to the fish. Season with additional salt and pepper as needed. Garnish with cilantro.

While the fish is cooking, heat the tortillas. Keep them warm in a towel or a warming dish. Arrange the avocado, orange segments, shredded lettuce, and green onion in small bowls.

To serve, place a spoonful of the snapper and sauce onto warm tortillas and garnish with the remaining ingredients and hot sauce, if desired. Serve immediately.

# Old New England–Style Cod Casserole

Seafood alternatives: Salmon, Pacific Snapper

Inspired by the wonderful book *Cod* by Mark Kurlansky, this recipe is adapted from a traditional chowder recipe from Boston, circa 1829. It is a nice change from plain scalloped potatoes.

**Serves 6**

3 to 4 pounds russet potatoes, peeled and thinly sliced

4 tablespoons butter or margarine

4 tablespoons flour

1 teaspoon salt

1 teaspoon freshly ground black pepper

2 pounds boneless cod fillet, sliced into 1/2-inch-thick pieces

6 slices lean bacon or ham, fried crisp and drained (optional)

1 cup minced onion

1/2 teaspoon dried thyme

2 cups milk or cream

1 cup crushed oyster crackers, pilot bread, or chowder crackers

Preheat the oven to 350°.

Butter a 9 by 13-inch casserole or oval baking dish.

Neatly arrange a layer of potatoes on the bottom of the baking dish. Dot with butter and dust with flour. Season with salt and pepper. Top with half of the cod, bacon, onion, and thyme. Repeat with another layer of potatoes, butter, and flour, then with the remaining cod, bacon, onion, and thyme. Finish with a layer of potato.

Pour the milk in along the edge of the pan. Top with the crushed crackers and dot with any remaining butter. Bake in the oven for 1 hour, or until the potatoes are tender and the top is golden brown.

Remove from the oven and let rest for 10 minutes before serving.

# Halibut Ho!

DRIFTING IN A HEAVY SEA 50 miles off Alaska's Kodiak Island, waiting for high noon, the hour of the halibut. Dozens of boats circle the area like sharks, waiting for the noon opening, ready to unleash thousands of hooks on some 40 million pounds of halibut, the annual quota for this region. For the state of Alaska: another 60 million pounds. You can almost feel them under the keel: Pacific halibut, *Hippoglossus stenolepis,* "hippos of the sea."

*"Five minutes!"*

Eighty "skates" of gear are baited and ready. With a skate equaling 1,800 feet, that's 25 miles of line—16,000 baited hooks—stretching across the bottom of the sea. Multiply that by the other boats, enough baited gear to reach China!

*"Let 'er rip!"*

Coils of baited hooks sizzle over the side, gulls wheeling and diving after the bait slapping the surface, then disappearing into the depths. Setting is the easy part. The hard part is hauling it back—especially with 50,000 pounds of halibut hanging on the line! If we're lucky, maybe more.

*"Flag!"*

After four hours of "soak time," the time the bait is left on the bottom, we're hauling it back aboard the boat. I can see the hooks coming up—*empty, empty, empty.* A "chicken" comes up, a halibut smaller than 20 pounds. Most of these fish will range from 20 to 40 pounds—called "mediums."

*"Whale!"*

A big one. A whale is a halibut more than a hundred pounds. It takes two of us to haul it over the rail. Only the females get this big because they live longer—up to 50 years, compared to 15 years for the males. We turn her over on her back, white-side up, to keep her from thrashing. An old halibut trick.

Larger fish are just as tasty as the smaller ones, but whatever the size, you want to buy halibut fresh. You want to buy any fish fresh if you can, but for some species— swordfish, tuna, cod, salmon—the difference between fresh and frozen is not that great if the freezing is done properly. With halibut, it is. A very lean fish, any dehydration at all in the freezer and it will lose its natural moisture.

Luckily, fresh halibut is now available from November to May. In the old "derby" fishery (back when I fished for halibut), the entire annual quota (of some 60 million pounds) was harvested in one or two 24-hour openings, forcing processors to freeze most of it because there weren't enough planes to fly it out fresh. Those days are gone.

But even fresh halibut can turn to sawdust in your mouth if you're not careful. The idea is to keep it moist and not overcook it. Here's an old halibut fisherman's trick that can't be beat—the way we cooked it on the boat. Slather the fillets (nice and thick) with mayonnaise (you can use lowfat mayonnaise if you like), a sprinkle of tarragon or dill (whatever you like), salt, and pepper, then wrap them in foil—and into the oven they go. Primitive, but it works. The mayonnaise, which has a delicate, subtle flavor, helps retain moisture—even adds moisture.

How long do you cook it? Forget all those cooking formulas for fish (every fish is different). Test it with a fork. When the fish is just about to reach a full flake—that is, begins to lose its translucency and fall apart—quickly remove it from the heat and serve.

*"Clean 'em and ice 'em!"*

There's no leaving fish hanging around on deck in this fishery. It's one of the cleanest, most quality-oriented (and biologically responsible) fisheries in the world. A big statement, but true. Almost all the harvest (90 percent) comes from the cold, clean waters of Alaska, harvested entirely by longline gear (no nets dragging across the bottom), each fish brought aboard the boat one at a time, still alive, bled and cleaned and iced immediately.

As for biologically responsible, this is the only fishery I know that is managed by scientists—the International Pacific Halibut Commission—who put the health of the resource first, not theoretically, but in actual practice. Scientists don't recommend (to politicians who make the decisions), they *rule*. Consider the sad case of the Atlantic halibut, once a thriving species, but overfished by trawlers (along with haddock and cod). There's no returning undersized halibut in a trawl fishery; everything comes up dead, or as good as dead. Even their habitat is left in rubble. In Alaska, trawlers are not allowed to keep halibut, and what halibut they do catch (accidental bycatch) is severely restricted, every fish counted by a federal observer, and when the aggregate limit is reached, the entire fishery is closed down. The result: Pacific halibut is thriving.

Such beautiful fish! You only see their white skin (the underside) in the fish market, but their backs are a stunning image of the ocean floor, intricate beyond belief. Of course, when they die, it fades away, but when you see them fresh out of the water, as we did, it leaves you with a very powerful image: that the bottom of the sea, itself, is a living thing.

Now, to get back to fishing. You can't be thinking about this aesthetic crap when you're fishing. Give me the gaff! We had a big one alongside. Up and over, bleed 'em and gut 'em and into the fish-hold it goes. The line keeps coming in, hook after hook.

If you were there on deck you might have picked up a useful idea or two. For example why were the fishermen cutting into the halibut heads? An ancient Norwegian ritual? Yes! Those Norwegians know their fish. We were carving out the halibut cheeks and stashing them in boxes with our names on them. Homepacks. We sold the halibut, but we kept the cheeks. Truly a delicacy. In fact, you may have eaten them without knowing it. Unscrupulous restaurants have substituted them for crab meat for years. If you see them for sale, go for it! But make sure there are no signs of yellowing (an indication of tired, probably frozen product). Very delicate, very tasty—and no bones.

The trip I'm revisiting here was in 1991, the last year of the crazy derby system that I mentioned earlier: the entire annual quota taken in a couple of short 24-hour openings. (It was as though the Halibut Commission couldn't stand having you fish for their halibut more than a few days.) Anyway, when it was over, we had 35,000 pounds of halibut aboard—in one day's fishing. The crew of seven devoured the dinner I made for them (halibut, naturally) and disappeared into their bunks, leaving me with the dishes and the wheel watch. Fair enough. I watched while they worked.

Kodiak Island was off my port side, the sea as flat as a flounder, just me and a lot of snoring from below deck. The *Yakutat* was the name of the boat, a 60-foot halibut schooner that's been fishing these waters since 1913. The spokes on the helm were worn down from hundreds of hands, and I thought about all those Norwegians who stood here in my place for all those years. It made me yawn.

The next day we unloaded our catch in Cordova. The fish looked beautiful, and we felt proud to deliver them. By the next day, they'd be in Seattle and then to points around the country. In the old days, the boats would make the run down to Seattle to sell their fish, and the halibut would be unloaded and shipped by train as far away as New York and Boston. And they called it "fresh"!

On the plane back to the "Lower 48," I read about the halibut opening in the newspaper: *"In just two 24-hour openings . . . U.S. longliners harvested 43 million pounds—about a million pounds an hour."* No wonder I was tired. My conclusion from the trip? Two things. First, sanity sometimes prevails, as in the case of the halibut fishery; and second, eat all the halibut you can. You can't find a better fish or one from purer waters than the . . . *zzzzzzzzzzz.*

# Halibut Marinated in Mustard and Rosemary

Seafood alternatives: Salmon, Cod, Halibut Cheeks, Sturgeon

This fish will receive raves. The marinade is one of those all-purpose recipes you find yourself keeping in your fridge as a staple. Any leftover cold fish makes a great sandwich or salad.

| Serves 6 |
| --- |

**Marinade**

1/2 cup olive oil

1/4 cup coarse-grain mustard

3 tablespoons cider vinegar

3 tablespoons chopped fresh parsley

2 tablespoons horseradish

2 teaspoons chopped fresh rosemary

2 cloves garlic, minced

1/2 teaspoon salt

1/2 teaspoon freshly ground black pepper

6 (6 to 8-ounce) halibut fillets or steaks

2 tablespoons olive oil

Combine the olive oil, mustard, vinegar, parsley, horseradish, rosemary, garlic, salt, and pepper until well mixed. Add the fish and gently stir to coat. Marinate for up to 24 hours.

To cook, sear the fish in olive oil over medium-high to high heat for 4 minutes on each side. The halibut will be golden brown and just opaque through. Serve immediately.

# Grilled Halibut with Oregano and Fennel

Seafood alternatives: Sturgeon, Tuna, Swordfish, Lobster

Halibut is a dry fish, so it is often buried under a lot of sauce. Here, fresh fish is marinated in clean, simple flavors, and then grilled over hot coals just long enough to be tender. The flavor and texture of the halibut is delicately enhanced by the infusion of Mediterranean flavors. Serve the halibut with bowls of olives and slices of perfect summer tomatoes for a healthy summer meal.

## Serves 4

1 onion, sliced into rounds

4 (6 to 8-ounce) halibut steaks or fillets

2 cloves garlic, minced or pressed

1 1/2 tablespoons chopped fresh oregano, or 2 teaspoons dried

1 bulb fresh fennel, sliced through the root into 1/4-inch slabs

1 lemon, sliced

2 tablespoons extra virgin olive oil

1/4 teaspoon salt plus more to taste

1/4 teaspoon freshly ground black pepper plus more to taste

Lemon wedges for garnish

Oregano sprigs for garnish

Place the slices of onion in a large, shallow, nonmetallic dish. Arrange the halibut steaks on the onion and sprinkle with the garlic and oregano. Top with the fennel and slices of lemon, and drizzle with the olive oil. Cover with plastic wrap and marinate in the refrigerator for at least 4 hours or, preferably, overnight.

Preheat an outdoor grill.

Remove the slices of fennel and onion from the dish and grill them until they are lightly charred and tender, about 12 to 14 minutes. Remove the vegetables from the grill and cut the cores from the fennel. Discard the cores and toss the onion and fennel together with 1/4 teaspoon salt and 1/4 teaspoon pepper, and arrange onto a serving dish.

Grill the halibut steaks until they are just opaque through, about 4 minutes on each side. Season the steaks with salt and pepper to taste and place on the cooked vegetables. Garnish the fish with lemon wedges and oregano sprigs. Serve immediately.

# Fresh from the Hook!

IT'S GETTING CLOSE TO FISHING SEASON. Of course, it's always fishing season somewhere, but I'm talking about *my* fishing season. Every summer I go to Alaska to revisit my past life as a commercial salmon fisherman. What I remember are those wonderful days when I caught lots of fish, the weather was fine, the engine didn't miss a stroke, and I was the captain of my destiny.

What I forget is that those days never existed. Fishing is really long hours of mind-bending monotony mitigated by moments of sheer terror. I know this, but I always go back for more.

Last year, I went to Craig, a small fishing village on the seaward side of Prince of Wales Island in southeast Alaska. I arrived by floatplane, my sea bag bulging with woolen sweaters, rain gear, and a pair of rubber boots. Even though it was July, I knew the weather would be miserable because it always is. I've fished there when it rained so hard you could see a layer of freshwater on the surface of the ocean.

I was met at the dock by my brother, Gary, who's been fishing here for 30 years. Like many small-boat fishermen up there, he has to fish for a variety of species to make ends meet: salmon, halibut, lingcod, yelloweye rockfish, dogfish (that he sells for shrimp bait), almost anything that comes up on a hook. We got my gear aboard his boat, a 29-foot combination troller-longliner, iced up, and disappeared into the mists of Sea Otter Sound.

That night, after a long day, we anchored off Port Alice, where we listened to the weather report over the VHF radio. *"Small craft advisories . . . gusts up to 30 knots."*

Never fails. We were in for a blow in the morning, but right then we had some rock cod fillets on the grill . . . and the present time is all that matters when you're fishing. Rock cod (actually a rockfish, not a cod—*Sebastes caurinus*) are a fish you see in live tanks in Asian markets and restaurants all along the Pacific Coast, especially in Vancouver B.C., where fishermen cater to the live-fish trade. The Chinese will always serve this fish whole (they don't get much bigger than a pound), but the fillets, with a little ginger and soy, were excellent as well. Then to bed.

At first light, we pulled anchor and lowered the trolling gear. I had the port line, my brother had the starboard. Here's a snapshot of what we were doing: dragging two wire lines behind the boat, each weighted down with a 30-pound lead "cannon ball." On each line, dozens of lures were attached on short leaders (called "spreads") and trolled behind the boat to catch salmon. What you probably know about troll salmon is that it costs a premium in the market. Now you'll know why.

*Fish on!*

The bell on the starboard trolling pole was jingling frantically, signaling we had a fish on. Gary hauled the salmon—a spunky silver—to the surface with a hydraulic reel then reached over the side and gave it a well-placed tap on the head with the gaff and gently lifted it into the boat.

And so it went, plucking salmon off the hooks like ears of corn, one after another. No battering themselves on deck until they were dead, bruising their flesh and traumatizing the fish. A little tap on the head and the salmon dies with a smile on its face. The happier the salmon, the better the quality. Bruising means soft flesh and rapid spoilage. Plus, it's not a nice way to let a salmon die.

Here's the key point: *How* a fish is caught determines its quality. How it's handled *after* it's caught is the next crucial step.

Once in the boat, the salmon is immediately bled (by slitting a gill raker) and left undisturbed while it goes through *rigor* (otherwise the flesh will tighten up and turn tough). Some trollers will go so far as to place the salmon on a special mat to protect it against any scale loss. Too many missing scales is always a sign of poorly handled fish. As fish buyers are always preaching to fishermen: "We can't make a fish any better than it is after we get it."

What I like about hook-and-line fishing is that the fish are handled one at a time, not as a clump of flesh in a net. Handcrafted seafood is what it amounts to, but it's not always practical. If the tuna that goes into the can had to be caught on hook-and-line, the cost would go through the roof. One at a time is very labor intensive; bringing fish up tons at a time in a seine or trawl net isn't.

I also favor hooks for conservation reasons. It's much easier to target particular species and size groups (and exclude others) by regulating hook size, type of bait, fishing depth, and so on than it is with nets—although regulating mesh size helps. The other thing about hooks is you can release juvenile or protected species live, not so easy with nets. On the other hand, one of the dirtiest fisheries I've ever seen was the monofilament longline fishery off Florida for swordfish—hooks fished off surface longlines—and one of the cleanest was the Copper River gillnet fishery in Alaska. To be fair, it has to be taken on a case-by-case basis.

Time to ice the salmon. This is a job I hate because before long you begin to feel like a frozen fish. So down I went into the fish-hold. The temperature down there is just a little above freezing. On each side there are bins filled with flake ice. Each salmon has to be "belly-poked" with ice (a handful of ice placed in the belly cavity) and then stacked in one of the bins, each salmon completely buried in ice.

On some boats, the fish are separated by species, especially if the troller is doing direct marketing. Which brings me to my last point about fish quality: species. Treat a king salmon and a pink salmon exactly the same, cook them exactly the same, and the difference will be tremendous. (And, for that reason, so will the price.)

Here's a quick lesson in salmon species. All things being equal, the king salmon and the sockeye salmon are the very best to eat (some favor one, some favor the other), followed by the silver salmon and then the chum salmon. What about farmed salmon? That's like comparing chickens to pheasant. The price is right, though.

The fish all iced, I climbed out of the fish-hold and thawed my hands over the stove in the wheelhouse. Already there were more salmon on deck waiting to be stored below. First, a cup of coffee. Through the window, I could see the sky darkening, and it was not even noon yet. We were in for a blow, but right then I was content: at one with all the other critters around there—bears, eagles, foxes, sea lions, killer whales—all obsessed with the same burning idea: a salmon dinner.

Or, for that matter, a salmon *lunch*. You never want to face a bad blow on an empty stomach.

# Smoked Salmon Hash

Seafood alternatives: Cooked Salmon, Smoked Trout, Smoked Oysters

This hash is the perfect dish for holiday or weekend brunches. It also makes a great dinner. The hash is tasty on its own, but it is even better when topped with a fried egg just like its corned beef cousin. Use a good quality hot-smoked or kippered salmon.

### Serves 4

2 to 3 tablespoons vegetable oil

1¹/₂ pounds Yukon Gold or other waxy potato, diced

1 cup diced onion

1 cup peeled and diced carrot

¹/₂ cup diced rutabaga

¹/₂ cup diced parsnip

1 clove garlic, minced

¹/₄ teaspoon dried sage

¹/₄ teaspoon dried thyme

¹/₄ teaspoon salt

¹/₄ teaspoon freshly ground black pepper

8 ounces smoked salmon, skinned and broken into large chunks

4 eggs (optional)

Heat a large skillet over medium-high heat. Swirl in the oil and add the potato and onion. Cook, stirring regularly, until the potato begins to soften, about 5 minutes. Add the carrot, rutabaga, parsnip, and garlic. Sprinkle in the sage and thyme. Decrease the heat to medium and cook, stirring regularly, until the potato is crisp and brown, 20 to 25 minutes.

Season with salt and pepper. Add the smoked salmon and cook another 2 to 3 minutes, stirring gently, until the salmon is evenly distributed and warmed through. Serve the hash warm, topped with a fried egg.

# Walnut and Horseradish-Crusted Salmon Fillets

Seafood alternatives: Bluefish, Arctic Char, Sturgeon

Salmon is a fish that can really stand up to robust, earthy flavors. Although the amount of horseradish seems excessive at first, it mellows and adds a gentle complexity to the fish. This is a nice cold-weather dish, served with roasted winter squash and hearty greens.

## Serves 6

1½ cups walnut pieces

2 tablespoons chopped fresh, tender herbs (such as tarragon, parsley, chives, or chervil)

6 (6-ounce) salmon fillets, skin on, pin bones removed

4 tablespoons horseradish

½ teaspoon salt

½ teaspoon freshly ground black pepper

¼ cup butter, melted

Coarsely chop the walnuts. Mix the nuts and the herbs and set aside while you prepare the salmon.

Place the salmon fillets on a lightly oiled baking sheet. Spread the horseradish evenly over the fish and season with salt and pepper. Divide the nut mixture onto the fillets and press gently. Drizzle with the melted butter. The fish can be prepared to this point and kept refrigerated for 24 hours.

Preheat the oven to 425°.

Bake the fillets for 10 to 12 minutes until the nuts are brown and the fish is resilient when pressed at the thickest part.

Lift from the baking sheet. Serve immediately.

# Dinner with Devon

I WAS ON A BEACH IN MEXICO with my fishing partner. Devon is his name. He's quite a character. He has flaming red hair, three teeth (two on top, one on the bottom), and walks like a sailor, swaggering from side to side with a bottle in his hand.

He's a person of few teeth and fewer words. I normally value a fishing partner of few words, except in his case he repeats the same ones over and over (whether I listen or not). One of his favorite words is *numm,* roughly the equivalent of "fish," of which he is a great connoisseur. Sitting high in his favorite chair, he'll not only repeat the sound—*numm-numm-numm*—but accompany it with a loud banging of his spoon. "Tuna and Timpani," I call it.

My grandson and I, for so he is, were there on vacation. His mother was there, too, but right then she was taking a long (solitary) walk on the beach. I hoped she would come back soon. Fishing with Little Red—some people would call it baby-sitting, but there's no "sitting" with this guy—can be a challenge. One nice thing about being a grandpa, though, is when his mother comes back, I'm off the hook. I can head to the lounge for a margarita, perhaps two margaritas, depending on how the "fishing" went.

Vacations are always a good time for reflection, and one of mine, as I sat there numming it up with my grandson, was why more children don't eat seafood? Not only is it highly nutritious, easily digested, and with virtually no saturated fat, but if it's introduced in the right way, children love it. And if you call it "hamburger," they can't get enough of it.

In fact, you can fairly describe fish as "mother's milk." Here's the proof. What do fish and breast milk have in common? The answer is omega-3 fatty acid. Omega-3—of which seafood is an abundant source—is also present in breast milk. My daughter (Little Red's mom) let this fact drop in a conversation the other day. I was delighted to hear it, but not surprised. Researchers have attributed just about every health benefit imaginable to omega-3 (from preventing heart disease to improving your complexion); that it would be in mother's milk seems like just the kind of smart thing Mother Nature would do.

And she did. Eileen Paul, a nutritionist for Group Health in Seattle, estimates breast milk contains "about 1 percent omega-3 by weight." Formula milk, on the other hand, has no omega-3—not naturally, in any case. Paul told me that baby food companies sometimes add it to hype their product (although, after examining several major labels, I saw no omega-3 listed).

What exactly does omega-3 do for babies? Most of the nutritionists I talked to believe its value is in *prevention,* not nutrition. (One nutritionist told me that omega-3 from sardines is now being used to boost the immune systems of HIV patients.)

What I wanted to know is if seafood is "mother's milk" to babies (so to speak), why don't any of the baby food companies include it in their products? If babies can have beef stew and macaroni and cheese, why can't they have pâté of pompano?

So—to get back to my reflection—I called Gerber. "Where's the fish?" I asked. "In France," they answered. They produce it for European babies, but not for the babies in the U.S.

*"Pourquoi?"* I asked.

"The smell and taste are too strong for the market," said Nancy Lindner, manager of public relations. Apparently, fish failed the baby taste tests in the United States—but babies in France passed it.

This didn't make sense. "Do babies in France eat it with capers and white wine?"

"No," said Lindner, "with vegetables."

What does this mean? That even French *babies* know more about food than we do? Nonsense. Little Red loves almost any kind of seafood, especially if you sprinkle a little sand on it. Right now he's foraging for it on the beach—bits of seaweed, dead clams, crab shells—all going into his mouth. My fingers are constantly digging them out, a dangerous operation even with only three teeth. Where was his mother anyway? She seemed to have disappeared over the horizon.

Seafood requires a little education. The tastes are more complex than, say, macaroni and cheese. But a piece of fish lightly sautéed with perhaps a touch of tarragon has Little Red hammering on his high chair with gusto, *numm-numm, BANG! BANG!*

In general, whiter-fleshed species are preferred over darker-fleshed because the taste is milder. I recommend catfish, halibut, haddock, cod, sole, and sea bass just for starters—all skinless, boneless fillets, of course. Avoid any kind of shellfish, though. Some children will have an allergic reaction. As far as food safety is concerned, seafood has an excellent record if you exclude raw oysters. Oysters on the half shell for kids is not a good idea. I'm sure the kids would agree.

And here's a good tip from Grandpa. Never serve a toddler fish on a plate. The result is always the same: "Fish Frisbee." Instead, I cut it up carefully on a tray, making sure that it's cooked thoroughly and that any bones or skin are removed. Undercooked fish doesn't pose the same risk as, say, undercooked chicken, but it's best to cook it until it's well done.

Speaking of seafood—wait, I got a bite! I reeled in the fish, a small snapper, and started cleaning it on the beach. We were staying at the Palmilla Hotel (in Los Cabos), where the chefs are very happy to cook our catch and are familiar with Little Red's gustatory enthusiasm.

I set the heart and innards aside and started filleting the fish. The heart was still beating, which is not unusual. This might seem "gross" to some readers, but I believe children should take responsibility early for what they eat. (Chickens have hearts, too—as in the expression, "chicken-hearted.")

I put the fillets in the bucket, but when I went to toss away the rest, the heart was not only not beating, it wasn't there. I looked around quickly for Little Red's mother. Luckily, she was still out of sight. "How was it?" I asked.

*Numm!*

# Sole Mornay (a.k.a. Cheesy Fish!)

Seafood alternatives: Cod, Turbot, Halibut

White fish in cheese sauce—what more could a kid want? The only way to make this dish even better, is to sprinkle it with fish-shaped crackers just before you serve it. This is a recipe that grown-ups will love too. If the suggested imported cheese is a little sophisticated for your toddler, feel free to use their favorite neon orange cheese sauce instead. Just do whatever it takes to get your kids to eat wholesome seafood.

### Serves 6

2 tablespoons butter or margarine

2 tablespoons flour

1$^1$/$_2$ cups plus 2 tablespoons milk

$^1$/$_2$ teaspoon salt

$^1$/$_4$ teaspoon freshly ground black pepper

$^1$/$_4$ teaspoon dry mustard

Pinch of ground cayenne pepper (optional)

Melt the butter in a saucepan. Remove the pan from the heat and stir in the flour. Cook, stirring constantly until the flour and butter are a light golden brown, about 2 minutes. This thin paste is called a roux.

In separate pan, scald the 1$^1$/$_2$ cups milk. Pour the steaming milk into the roux, whisking constantly to prevent lumps from forming. Continue stirring over medium heat for 3 to 4 minutes, until the sauce bubbles and thickens enough to coat the back of the spoon. Remove the sauce from the heat and stir in the salt, pepper, mustard, cayenne, and cheese. If you are not using the sauce immediately, place a piece of plastic wrap directly onto the surface of the sauce to prevent a skin from forming. Set aside or chill until ready to use.

(continued)

(continued from page 183)

**1 cup grated cheese (Gruyère or a good-quality white Cheddar is best, Parmesan, fontina, or Gouda also work well)**

**1½ pounds sole fillets**

**1 cup of goldfish-shaped crackers**

Preheat the oven to 325°.

Lightly grease a casserole or baking dish.

Fold the thin ends of the sole fillets under so they are an even thickness throughout. Oven poach the fillets by placing them with the 2 tablespoons milk in the prepared dish. Cover with a square of buttered parchment paper or foil. Bake for 10 to 12 minutes until the sole is cooked on the sides, but still slightly translucent in the center.

Remove the fish from the oven and pour the juices from the pan into the prepared sauce.

Preheat the broiler.

Pat the fish dry with a paper towel. Spoon the cheese sauce over the sole fillets. Broil until the cheese sauce is lightly brown and bubbly, about 2 minutes.

Sprinkle the fish with goldfish crackers or additional cheese and serve warm.

# Snapper in Saltines

Seafood alternatives: Cod, Red Snapper, Catfish, Tilapia, Any Other Mild Whitefish

Seafood doesn't always have to be sophisticated. This is a dinner staple in regular rotation in many American families. And once you have tried it, you may find yourself craving it as often as the kids do! To employ the little ones in the kitchen, let them smash up the crackers. They love it.

## Serves 4

1 pound snapper fillets

1/2 cup all-purpose flour

1/4 teaspoon salt

1/8 teaspoon freshly ground black pepper

2 eggs

2 cups saltine crumbs (about 50 crackers, placed in a resealable bag and finely crushed)

2 to 3 tablespoons vegetable oil

Lemon wedges for garnish

Tartar sauce

Ketchup

Carefully run your hands along the fish fillets to feel where the bones are. Using a sharp knife, remove the strip of flesh in which any bones might be. Cut the remaining fish into strips.

Season the flour with the salt and pepper. Toss the fish strips in the flour, patting to remove any excess. Then dip the strips in the egg and then in the saltine crumbs. Panfry the fillets a few at a time over medium heat in a tablespoon of oil, turning once, until the fish is cooked through and golden brown, about 3 minutes. Wipe out the pan and add new oil if the crumbs begin to burn.

Transfer strips to a platter and serve warm with lemon wedges, tartar sauce, and yes, even ketchup.

# Bangkok:
# A Tale of Culinary Intrigue

 "MY HAPPINESS IS YOUR HAPPINESS," said my host, Mr. Suvisist Dilokvilas. He and his business partner, Mr. Vason Matinon, had taken me out to dinner, and Mr. Dilokvilas was showing me the secret of eating barbecued shrimp.

"This is the best part," he says, twisting off the head, exposing its mysteries. "First this sauce, then a little of that one . . . be careful of the seeds!" You *learn* to be careful of the seeds.

The shrimp reminded me of eating crawfish—suckin' heads—except these were more the size of baby lobster: giant freshwater prawns, *Macrobrachium rosenbergii*—in Thai, *koong yai*. Called *Choong Thord Grob Charw Wang* on the menu, they were accompanied with coconut rice and bathed in a sweet and sour tamarind sauce. The shells collected at the side of the plate as I quaffed them down with Singha, the local beer.

My friends (for so we became) were showing me the pleasures of Thai seafood. Thailand is famous for its farmed shrimp, almost all of which is exported out of the country (much of it to the United States). But it was *macrobrachia* and wild black tiger shrimp that they were serving in the restaurants along the Chao Phraya River,

186

looking you right in the eye from live tanks at almost every entrance. They not only liked their seafood fresh here, but still kicking.

Ahhh, the steamed pomfret! The pungent smells of cilantro, ginger, and garlic mixed with the ripening aroma of the river . . . *whew!* Pomfret is one of Thailand's favorite fish. It weighs only two or three pounds, and is a close relative of the pompano (a revered fish in Florida). It's almost always served whole—the best proof that it's a pomfret—steamed with lemongrass or garlic and ginger. And, of course, all the sauces, some of them smoking hot, that go with it. Not only sauces but sequences of sauces, this one first, that one second . . . different sauces for different fish.

Mr. Dilokvilas—"Please call me Khunpol," he insisted, forming his hands into a tent and bowing—was the managing director of Siam Bengal Resources Ltd., which supplied boats and fishermen to other countries. I knew his company from Saudi Arabia, where I had just been. My host there was Saudi Fisheries Company, one of Khunpol's major clients. I didn't go out on any of his boats, but I did spend a week shrimp trawling in the Red Sea on a Saudi-owned, Australian-built shrimp trawler crewed by South Koreans. Nothing is as simple as it seems out there.

Saudi Arabia was amazing. The country has built a "cold chain" across the desert, opening up the interior to fresh seafood. State-of-the-art processing plants, Mercedes Benz refrigerated trucks, one of the largest retail fish chains in the world, cadres of Scandinavian consultants—all part of the government's policy of self-sufficiency. I visited a lot of fish markets while I was there; in fact I had to dress up as a Saudi on one occasion because the fish market in Jiddah was close to a military base and there wasn't time to go through all the red tape to get in. So I disguised myself as an Arab, snapping pictures and slipping the roles of film to an "agent," who happened to be a member of the government.

What fun it was! I was telling the story to my friends who were very amused because they knew the man who put me up to it, Dr. Nasser Othman Al Saleh, president of Saudi Fisheries Company. The fish in the market had all these exotic names—hamoor, bohar, derak, ma'agub—but they were all my old friends (spotted grouper, red snapper, Spanish mackerel, little tuna). Then came the soldiers, surrounding me with machine guns. Pointed right at me. They took my camera and jerked the film out. I knew what they were thinking: an Israeli spy! "No, I'm a fish writer. I'm working for the Saudi government. It was their idea to dress me up like this . . . honest."

It was the good Dr. Nasser, in fact, who was paying for our dinner—and my hospitality—in Thailand for the next week. The way it was arranged, each night a different member of Khunpol's company took me out to dinner. I was dismayed to hear most of them didn't make it to work the next day, but I took it as a compliment.

"My pleasure is your pleasure," as Khunpol would say.

Now, it was Khunpol's turn to tell a story, about how he and Mr. Matinon had been wealthy entrepreneurs with more than 30 trawlers and more than a thousand fishermen, but they were "betrayed by a greedy sea captain."

The stories added spice to the food: stories of pirates, mysterious sinkings . . . betrayals. "I fell very far . . . only the faintest breath, sir, was left in me," said Khunpol, applying his knife to the pomfret with deftness. "Here, try this part," he said, "it's the tastiest." Every part is different.

I popped up from the pomfret long enough to take in my surroundings. Kaloang is not what you'd call one of Bangkok's "listed" restaurants. The name in English means "home kitchen," and that's what this was: home cooking. I asked my Thai friends to take me to restaurants *they* liked—"where the food was very good, but not necessarily great"—and this was it. (I admit to being suspicious of two things: food for tourists and food for posterity.)

Kaloang is built on pilings and extends out over the water with a view of the river traffic. A man in a small sampan was hawking dried squid just below us, as if we didn't have enough to eat already. Squid is a staple in Thailand, very cheap and prepared masterfully, even by sidewalk vendors who cook it in the gutters over hot coals. Some of them have occupied the same spot for years, a venerable restaurant in the street.

The sun was sinking below the horizon bathing us in the afterglow of a Southeast Asia sunset. It was very busy now, food pouring out of the kitchen in an endless parade of marvelous seafood: 14 shrimp dishes alone; seven crab dishes—more than 80 dishes in all on the menu, not including soups or specialties such as "Softshell Turtle in Red Syrup" or "Boiled Serpent Head in Chile Soup." How could these people eat so much and be so skinny?

And what was a serpent head? Or a Sam-Lee fish? The menu was an intrigue in itself: "Eel in Curry with Chile," "Boiled Dryfish in Chile Soup," "Steamed Butterfish with Lemon," "Serpent Head Belly Cooked in Soup with Chile," "Fried Frog with Chile," "Pepper Sauce with Threadfin Fish . . ." The food was like Southeast Asia itself, intriguing and complex, nothing quite what it seemed, like the beautiful waitresses, whose faces seemed to hold some secret.

"Boys," said Khunpol, smiling.

"What?"

"The waitresses are boys."

"No."

"Boys dressed up as waitresses. This is the girls' night off."

I was a long way from Seattle, Washington.

The pomfret was superb: subtle and moist, the taste sharpened by the ubiquitous fish sauce *(nam pla)* made from fermented fish. I later checked out the pomfret at the local wholesale fish market. There are two species, the favored being the white pomfret, *Pampus argenteus,* because of its higher fat content. I looked at the auction prices, and it went for more than three times the price of the local snapper.

"When our fishing adventure is over"—Khunpol had a big fish deal pending with Saudi Arabia—"I'm going to shave my head and eyebrows and return to the jungle."

"Why that?" I asked, sucking a bone.

"Because in the jungle there is peace. In the fish business, there is none," he said.

The jungle, as it turned out, is where his company was born—in Laos and

Cambodia during the Vietnam War. The gentle Khunpol, it seemed, had been a jungle commando working for the CIA, and the soft-spoken Mr. Matinon was his supply officer. "We were working for the CIA, sir, but we were fighting for Thailand," said Khunpol.

The pomfret was reduced to a lingering whiff of cilantro, and on came the crab, smothered in an incredible yellow bean sauce. Mudcrab, *Scylla serrata:* I selected it myself from the live-tank as we entered the restaurant. At Chao-Sua, a Chinese restaurant where I later went for shark-fin soup—"It will make us very strong," said my host for that evening—the "menu" was literally swimming in front of the restaurant in tanks, a seafood host (wearing a tuxedo) was there to greet us and answer any of our questions. In one restaurant I went to, I was given a shopping cart to select the vegetables I wanted with my seafood, then picked out the seafood from a corridor of live tanks, which was scooped out and cooked in front of my eyes along with the vegetables.

"Another Singha please!" I was still licking my lips from the mudcrab when the stuffed horseshoe crab arrived, an inverted helmet of steamy seafood secrets enveloping us in its aroma. Such seafood!

Such appetites! Khunpol told me an average Thai will eat up to six times a day, but you'd have to look long and hard to see anyone here overweight. Lots of seafood and vegetables, very little meat.

"My happiness is your happiness," saluted Khunpol, and I saluted him back.

"Your happiness is my happiness," and we saluted again, both of us very happy. Surely, I thought, this is the happiest food on earth.

# Spicy Thai Clam Soup

Chowder is not the only kind of clam soup. Those who are familiar with Thai cooking should have most of these ingredients tucked in the pantry. If not, galangal, lemongrass, Thai curry paste, coconut milk, lime leaves, and fish sauce are available at better supermarkets. They can also be ordered through a good international foods catalog or Website.

## Serves 4

2 pounds small clams, well scrubbed

2 teaspoons peanut oil or vegetable oil

2 cloves garlic, chopped

1 teaspoon chopped fresh ginger, or 1 to 2 slices galangal root

2 tablespoons diced onion

1 stalk lemongrass, cut into long pieces and smashed with the side of a knife

1 heaping teaspoon Thai red curry paste

1/2 cup coconut milk

4 cups fish stock or clam nectar

Steam the clams open in two cups of water. Throw away any clams that remain tightly closed. Reserve the liquid and add fish stock or clam nectar to make 6 cups. Set the clams and the liquid aside.

(continued)

(continued from page 191)

1/2 cup Thai basil leaves, loosely packed

3 tablespoons fish sauce

3 tablespoons freshly squeezed lime juice

2 lime leaves

2 teaspoons sugar

Salt

Freshly ground black pepper

Cilantro for garnish

Sliced green onions for garnish

Heat the oil in a large saucepan. Add the garlic, ginger, onion, and lemongrass, and cook over medium heat until softened and aromatic, 3 to 4 minutes. Add the curry paste and stir. Whisk in the coconut milk and simmer until the mixture has separated, about 2 minutes more. Pour on the 6 cups of liquid. Add the basil, fish sauce, lime juice, lime leaves, and sugar. Season with salt and pepper to taste. Simmer for 5 minutes. Add the clams and garnish with cilantro and green onions. Serve immediately.

# Steamed Pomfret
# with Ginger and Cilantro

Seafood alternatives: Tilapia, Striped Bass, Sole, Trout

Virtually any seafood can be cooked in this manner. Arrange the fish or shellfish on a plate, sprinkle with aromatic herbs and seasonings, and steam to moist perfection. Few diets will exempt this healthy and flavorful presentation. White pomfret are available frozen at many international markets.

### Serves 2

2 white pomfret, cleaned

2 teaspoons chopped fresh, peeled ginger

2 to 3 cloves sliced garlic

1 to 2 minced Thai bird chiles, or 1 jalepeño, sliced thin

2 tablespoons fish sauce

2 tablespoons freshly squeezed lime juice

$1/2$ teaspoon salt

$1/2$ teaspoon ground black pepper

1 to 2 tablespoons chopped fresh cilantro

2 green onions, sliced

Place the pomfret on a dinner plate or platter. Fill each of the cavities with half of the ginger, garlic, and chiles. Sprinkle the fish sauce, lime juice, salt, and pepper evenly over the fish. Place the plate in a steamer or over an upturned bowl or rack in a wok. Steam the fish over gently boiling water for 8 to 10 minutes, or until the fish skin starts to peel back slightly at the gills and fins and the flesh is opaque through.

Remove the plate carefully and sprinkle the fish with cilantro and green onions. Serve immediately.

# Stir-Fried Squid with Asparagus and Basil

Seafood alternatives: Scallops, Shrimp, Tuna

This is a lightning quick stir-fry that is packed with the exotic flavors of Thailand. Thai curry paste and basil are now available at many supermarkets, and they can be found at international markets or mail-order sources.

| Serves 4 to 6 |
| :---: |

### Sauce

1/2 cup chicken broth or water

1 teaspoon Thai red curry paste

2 tablespoons soy sauce

2 tablespoons sugar

1 teaspoon cornstarch

8 ounces cleaned squid tubes and tentacles

2 tablespoons peanut oil

4 slices fresh ginger, about the size of a quarter

2 cloves garlic, chopped

To make the sauce, stir together the chicken broth, curry paste, soy sauce, sugar, and cornstarch. Set aside.

Cut the squid tubes into rings; halve the tentacles if they are large.

Preheat a wok or large skillet over medium-high heat.

Add half of the oil with the ginger slices. Cook until the ginger is aromatic and begins to brown, about 30 seconds. Discard the slices of ginger and add the squid, quickly tossing to coat in oil. Stir-fry until just firm, about 1 minute. Scoop out the squid and set aside on a plate.

1 green onion, white and green parts thinly sliced and kept separate

1¹/₂ pounds asparagus, trimmed into 1-inch lengths

1 tablespoon sherry

¹/₂ cup Thai basil leaves

Wipe out the wok and heat the remaining oil. Add the garlic and white of the onion, and cook quickly until aromatic, about 15 seconds. Add the asparagus and toss in the oil for 1 minute, or until the sizzling subsides. Add the sherry and continue to cook, tossing in the pan until the asparagus is just tender, about 3 minutes. Add the squid and the basil to the asparagus. Stir the sauce well and add to the wok. Cook, stirring constantly until the sauce has thickened and is shiny, about 1 minute.

Turn out onto a warm platter. Sprinkle with the remaining green onion and serve immediately.

# The Wages of Health

MY MISTAKE WAS getting a physical exam *before* I left for New Orleans. Otherwise, I wouldn't have arrived with a 293 handicap. My cholesterol count. Whatever else you might say about Cajun cuisine—that it's spicy, tasty, and generally sublime—you wouldn't say it was fat-free. Look at Paul Prudhomme.

Before going any further, I feel I should explain myself. I mean, what kind of fish writer has a high cholesterol count?

Blame it on my parents. Genetics did it. Rarely will I so much as dip a mussel or a clam in butter—and if I do (distracted by some deep thought), I barely get its little feet wet. But if one happens to fall into the bowl on the way to my mouth, what can I do but rescue it? Accidents happen.

As to sauces and such, I shun them. But if my sole is served with a cream sauce (the waiter forgot to hold it), I'll eat it anyway. I wouldn't want a nice piece of fish (I know it's under there somewhere) to go to waste.

I never eat anything with a French name, which always translates into calories. How do those French do it, anyway? They eat delicious (unhealthy) food, and they thrive. All they do for exercise is talk. Maybe it's all that wine they drink. Maybe that's my problem: I'm not drinking enough wine.

I arrived in the Big Easy under strict orders from my doctor not to have fun.

"Wudjadoinheeya?" asked the cab driver. He was taking me to my hotel from the airport. I guess I didn't look like a Baptist. They were everywhere. A big Baptist convention in town. "Shrimp, I'm here to write a story about Louisiana shrimp."

"Shwamps? Dey good!"

Cajun talk. These Louisianans love der shwamps.

At the hotel, I fought my way through the Baptists to get to the bar for a mint julep. A little whiskey cuts through cholesterol like a knife. I read that somewhere. Plus, you get some greens along with the whiskey. Healthy is the only way to go.

I won't take it upon myself to describe the restaurant scene in New Orleans. There are many books that do that very well. From a culinary standpoint, New Orleans is the Seafood Capital of America. It is also the Last Frontier of Fried. Ask a restaurant here if they "poach" their fish, they'll deny it and kick you out the door. They think poaching means illegal fishing.

What I needed was a culinary trainer. I called Karl Turner, executive director of the Louisiana Seafood Marketing and Promotion Board, and asked him if he'd take me out to dinner. What luck! He had reservations for us at the famous Emeril's—the hottest restaurant in town. The owner-chef, Emeril LaGasse, was on the tip of every culinary tongue in the country.

First, we had some work to do. Louisiana's shrimp industry was on its back, and I was there to take its pulse. "What's happening down here?" I asked. The answer was simple enough: *"Fahmed shwamp!"* Or *" 'em damned fahmed shwamp!"*

This was the early 1990s, when Southeast Asia's shrimp farms were really kicking in, flooding the United States with cheap shrimp, leaving Louisiana's shrimp industry in a lurch. The price of wild shrimp sank so low that many of the shrimp boats stayed tied to the dock. Many are still there. While Louisiana's shrimp production has remained amazingly steady at about 100 million pounds per year (to lead the nation), the number of boats fishing has been reduced by half.

And so it went from one plant to another all the way down to Grand Isle. Turner had borrowed a truck with a Louisiana Fish and Game logo on the side, which explained why all the bank fishermen were scattering as we drove through the bayous. By lunchtime my notebook was filled with vilification against the government, and I was weak with hunger. I hadn't caved in to any of the junk food that Karl kept bringing into the truck at every pit stop, chocolate donuts, Doritos in various flavors . . . and him as skinny as a rail.

So we went into a restaurant recommended by one of the shrimp processors I interviewed. A Caesar salad with maybe some boiled shrimp on top, I was thinking. But the closest thing to it was garlic shrimp "fried in butter." I could see my doctor frowning. I ordered a bowl of turtle soup instead, and Karl ordered the garlic shrimp.

We spent that afternoon talking to shrimpers. They were even more angry than the processors, but with them it was the detested TEDs (Turtle Excluder Devices), which they had to drag behind their boats to exclude turtles from their nets. "Dere ain't no turtles out dere anyway," I kept hearing, wondering about the turtle soup I had for lunch. The problem with TEDs, in addition to excluding nonexistent turtles, is that they excluded up to 20 percent of the shrimp. It was war. Blockades. Shots fired in the air. Sit-ins on the capitol steps in Baton Rouge. It was enough to make your stomach growl.

We arrived back in New Orleans in the evening, our ears ringing with rancor, and pulled up in front of Emeril's for dinner. The nonexistent-turtle soup that I had for lunch had worn off, and I was hungry for real food. We were greeted warmly at the door and led back to the kitchen, where we met Emeril LaGasse himself.

You can always tell the stature of a chef by the height of his hat. Emeril's was a serious fraction of his overall height. He was very gracious (although he talked with a suspiciously French accent), inviting us to order from his *special* menu. He smiled and ducked out the door to greet more of his guests. The place was packed.

The ambience of Emeril's reminded me more of Santa Monica than New Orleans. No one here was ordering "shwamps." Very sedate, everyone looking so . . . *slim.*

The first course arrived soon enough, then another and another. Smoked Gulf Shrimp Cake with Cucumber, Petite Shrimp and Cilantro Relish, Spicy Crab Cakes with Dipping Sauce, Barbecue Shrimp with Petite Biscuit. . . .

The recurring word was *petite*. Each serving was about the size of a silver dollar, arranged exquisitely at the center of the plate, whereupon I'd put on my reading glasses, admire it briefly, then scarf it down in a single bite.

The more I ate, the hungrier I got. That's the thing about healthy food, it always leaves you wanting more. (People eat all that fat for a reason.) This *nouveau* New Orleans food was killing me. I wanted something, anything, *not* healthy. I ordered the Savory Crawfish Cheesecake, guiltily gobbling it down. Now that was more like it!

Meanwhile, the bill arrived. It was the one thing about dinner that wasn't petite. It was close to $400—which is a lot of gumbo.

But it was worth the price. I learned three important lessons on that trip. First, the more fattening food you eat, the more you want. Second, the less fattening food you eat, the more you want. Third, the healthier the food, the more your stomach growls. The only way I know to have both—the pleasure of eating and the benefits of health—is to eat seafood. But don't eat it in New Orleans because you'll trade your diet to the devil. The food was just too good there. But, oh, what a last fling!

# Chile-Rubbed Mahimahi Salad

Seafood alternatives: Tuna, Snapper, Catfish, Shrimp

If you have good fish and lovely fruits and vegetables, there is no need for fancy techniques and complicated recipes. This salad can be served in countless variations. Season the fish with your favorite spice mixture and cook it to perfection. Then present the fillets on fresh greens with the season's best natural garnishes. Oranges, tomatoes, and chile powder are an especially nice combination.

### Serves 4

1 cup freshly squeezed orange juice

4 (6 to 8-ounce) mahimahi fillets

1 tablespoon chile powder

$^{1}/_{2}$ teaspoon coarse salt

1 tablespoon vegetable oil or light olive oil

2 bunches of watercress, cleaned and picked through (3 cups loosely packed leaves)

2 tomatoes, seeded and sliced

2 oranges, sectioned

Preheat the oven to 400°.

Pour the orange juice into a small saucepan. Simmer until the juice is reduced to a concentrated syrup, about 12 minutes.

Rub the fish with chile powder and coarse salt. Heat a large ovenproof skillet over medium-high heat and swirl in the vegetable oil. Sear the fish until it is nicely browned on one side, 4 minutes. Flip the fillets over and place the skillet in the oven to finish cooking, about 6 minutes more.

¹/₂ cup julienned jicama

1 tablespoon extra virgin olive oil

¹/₄ teaspoon salt

¹/₄ teaspoon freshly ground black pepper

2 green onions, sliced, for garnish

1 tablespoon chopped fresh cilantro for garnish

To assemble the salad, arrange the watercress on a serving platter. Scatter the tomatoes, orange sections, and jicama over the watercress. Place the fish on the prepared salad and pour over the olive oil and reduced orange juice. Season with salt and pepper, and garnish with green onions and cilantro. Serve immediately.

# Spicy Sundried Tomato Sauce

Use this big, bold vinaigrette as an alternative to mayonnaise or butter sauce. It is wonderful drizzled on smoked or grilled fish. Or use it as an alternative to a classic cocktail sauce. The flavors improve with time, so keep some on hand.

### Makes 1¹/₂ cups

1 cup diced tomato

¹/₄ cup red wine vinegar

2 tablespoons tomato paste

2 cloves garlic, minced

1¹/₂ teaspoons horseradish

1 teaspoon Dijon mustard

¹/₂ teaspoon crushed red chile flakes

¹/₂ teaspoon anchovy paste (optional)

¹/₄ cup extra virgin olive oil

¹/₂ teaspoon dried basil

¹/₄ teaspoon salt

Freshly ground black pepper

¹/₄ cup chopped, oil-packed sundried tomatoes

In a food processor or blender, purée the tomato, vinegar, tomato paste, garlic, horseradish, mustard, red chile flakes, and anchovy paste. Gradually blend in the olive oil. Season with the basil, salt, and pepper. Stir in the sun-dried tomatoes.

Keep in an airtight container in the refrigerator for up to a week.

# Crawfish Cornbread

Seafood alternatives: Shrimp, Rock Shrimp

The crawfish and vegetables are baked right into this cornbread. It is best made in a cast-iron skillet and served hot and crispy straight from the oven. If you don't own a skillet, mix the seared ingredients with the batter and place in a 10-inch round cake pan or an 8 by 8-inch brownie pan. This cornbread is also great for breakfast, brunches, or picnics.

### Serves 6

1 ½ cups cornmeal

1 cup flour

1 tablespoon baking powder

1 teaspoon salt

¼ teaspoon freshly ground black pepper

Pinch of ground cayenne pepper

1½ cups buttermilk

2 eggs

4 ounces spicy sausage meat (optional)

1 tablespoon vegetable oil

½ cup diced onion

½ cup diced, seeded green pepper

1 pound crawfish tail meat, chopped

Preheat the oven to 425°.

Mix the cornmeal, flour, baking powder, salt, pepper, and cayenne. Stir in the buttermilk and eggs until just combined. The batter will still be slightly lumpy.

Set the batter aside while you prepare the crawfish.

Heat a 10-inch, well-seasoned cast-iron skillet over medium-high heat and fry the sausage meat in the oil until it is brown and crisp. Add the onion and green peppers, and cook for 4 to 5 minutes until the vegetables are tender. Add the crawfish tails, and quickly toss and turn to sear.

Pour the contents of the skillet into the cornbread batter and stir just to mix. Then pour back into the hot pan. Bake for 20 to 25 minutes until the top is puffy and the bottom crust is crisp and brown.

Turn out the cornbread, cut into wedges, and serve hot or cold.

# Zen and the Art of Recipe Making:
# How Susan Volland Makes It Easy

RECIPES—THEY MAKE ME NERVOUS. Like "Paupiettes of Salmon with Mousse of Pike in Sorrel Sauce." I just saw it in a cookbook.

I was looking for something to whip together for lunch, but a recipe like that would take at least 17 sauté pans and a cadre of dishwashers to clean up after me. Plus a French-English dictionary to decode it.

Recipes are not always practical. They make great inspirational reading, but I usually end up like Frank Sinatra, "doing it my way," which is what makes me nervous. I always feel like *real* cooks follow recipes to the letter. "Spontaneous cooking" is what I do, but my wife calls it "anarchy in the kitchen." In any case, it was with some trepidation that I visited Susan Volland, creator of the recipes in this book, in her artist's loft in south Seattle the other day. The "art" she turns out is food. Recipe-testing is her business.

"Believe me, you're not alone," she laughed, as I sat down in her test kitchen, fessing up to my fears. She was putting together the Simple Stir-Fried Crab recipe as we talked, checking it for any miscues—such as a scallop recipe she tested recently in which the scallops were missing.

"But what about chefs? Surely they must—"

"Chefs communicate in grunts and shouts—that's the way they are when they cook. They don't remember their recipes in well-ordered sentences, and they always leave out things. What I do here is bridge the gap, putting their creations into recipes people can follow."

I was learning a lot. Apparently, there are those who know how to cook but *can't* compose a good recipe, and those who don't know how to cook but *can* compose a good recipe. Volland is one of the few who can do both, an award-winning chef on the one hand, a professional recipe-writer on the other.

"What are some of the common faults in recipes?" I asked.

"The recipe gives you the ingredients, but doesn't tell you how to use them.

"Recipes that are too vague. 'Cook until done,' which means what?

"Omitting key ingredients like salt and pepper.

"Including ingredients that are too hard to find—like flyingfish paste, boneless quail, foie gras. . . .

"Recipes that use terms most people don't know. I taught beginning cooking classes for a while, where some of the people in class didn't know the difference between simmer and boil. . . . A good recipe should be clear to anyone, even a beginner.

"Once you understand a recipe, you can begin to play with it, make it your own. That's where creativity enters into it and the fun begins."

As in the Simple Stir-Fried Crab now in progress. It was done in a matter of minutes—excellent, but even better (to my taste) when Susan added a spoonful of black bean sauce (not in the recipe) to give it some added zing.

Meanwhile, Susan's assistant, Ed Silver, was testing a mussel recipe (Spanish-Style Mussels with Olives), filling the kitchen with the smells of sherry, garlic, and marvelous *moules*. He was using rope-cultured mussels, the best, thin shells, uniform size (no barnacles), bursting with meat.

A big bowl of crab mousse (see page 34) was unveiled on the table and next to it a loaf of crunchy Italian bread.

It was lunchtime, and Susan's neighbors, a hungry band of furniture-makers, piano-tuners, and a commercial photographer, were drawn into the kitchen by the seashore smells, ready to do their duty as her happy guinea pigs. The Simple Stir-Fried Crab was already on the table ready to be judged. Let the tests begin!

The mousse was very delicate, an easy "A," slathered on chunks of crusty bread. The mussels were a little too complicated for me, a broth with a touch of white wine would have been more my style, but others gave them high scores. (Susan, I learned later, "adjusted" the recipe.) And, of course, the crab . . . so good . . . no need for melted butter with this recipe. Susan was using Dungeness crab, bought live, which she backed (removed the carapace) and cleaned in less than 15 seconds. (You can spare yourself the trouble by having your dealer do this for you.)

And the stories began. Nothing like seafood to generate conversation—which is part of the fun of eating it. Ask someone if they remember catching their first fish—and off you go! Or digging clams or catching crabs or raking mussels off the beach, usually with Mom or Dad or someone in the family who loved seafood—and loved catching it.

For Susan, it was her older brother, Mark, who showed her and her sister, Shelley, the tricks of harvesting from the sea—and her father, Roy Fowler, who taught her a few tricks in the kitchen. The family spent summers in a cabin in the Gulf Islands in British Columbia, where they lived off the sea, setting traps for spot shrimp (ripe with roe), trolling for salmon, trot lines baited with herring for whatever they could catch and put in the pot.

There was no hot water in the cabin, but all the "necessities" were there: a freezer chest stocked with smoked salmon, caviar, and herring for bait; a hundred-pound sack of wheat kernels for making bread. All the necessities, except one fateful summer Roy forgot the saffron.

"This was a major tragedy in his life," remembers Susan. His communal bouillabaisse was coming up. Invitations had been posted down on the fishing dock and around the island. Everyone was to bring something—cod, oysters, clams, mussels, crabs, shrimp, all to go into the communal pot. But no saffron! "We had to comb the entire island until we finally found some."

What we remember most are the simple dishes—clams with bacon and beer, homemade chowders, fresh salmon for breakfast, trout and eggs at a campsite on some lonely lake. . . . Just the idea of knowing the food you were eating.

Lost in our fish stories, the lunch hour slipped by quickly, and we all had to go back to work. Including me. Susan was putting together the ingredients for Orrechiette with Alaska King Crab and Chard. With the jury out, no one was left to do the tasting but me, which was okay. I was warming up to the idea of recipes as a creative process—one that required frequent tastings. After all, someone had to do it, and I was glad it was me. "Very good . . . but just a tad more king crab in the pasta, please."

# Simple Stir-Fried Crab

Seafood alternatives: Blue Crab, Lobster, Shrimp, Clams

A plain boiled or steamed crab served with melted butter can hardly be improved upon. But, with practice, this stir-fried crab can be prepared and served in less time than it takes to boil a pot of water. The aromatic crab is so simple it doesn't even need sauce. If you want to liven up the dish a bit, add 1/2 cup water and a heaping teaspoon of prepared black bean sauce, oyster sauce, or curry paste. If you would prefer not to deal with the mess of live crab, a good fishmonger will clean them for you, but you must cook them the day they are cleaned.

## Serves 2

1 or 2 live Dungeness crab (substitute cooked, cleaned crab if live are not available)

2 tablespoons peanut oil or vegetable oil

3 cloves garlic, sliced

1 teaspoon peeled, chopped fresh ginger

Pinch of crushed red chile flakes

2 to 3 tablespoons dry sherry or chicken stock

2 green onions, sliced

To clean a live crab, wear heavy-duty gloves. Gather up the legs and pinchers tightly in each hand, and then powerfully strike the belly of the crab against a sharp edge or corner. The edge of a dock or wharf is perfect for this. Once you strike the crab, immediately pull the legs together, away from the back shell. This is a wet, messy job. Discard the back and viscera. Using a cleaver, cut the crab into pieces. Crack the legs lightly with the back of the cleaver.

Heat a wok over high heat. Swirl in the oil. Add the garlic, ginger, red chile flakes, and crab. Toss and turn quickly using the sides of the wok to help distribute and cook the crab. Splash in the sherry and cover. Cook 5 to 6 minutes, stirring occasionally. (If you are using a cooked, cleaned crab, cook just until the crab is warmed through, 2 to 3 minutes.) When the crab is bright red and the meat can easily be extracted from the shell, sprinkle with green onions, stir well, and transfer to a warm serving platter.

Serve immediately with oversized napkins and fingerbowls.

# Spanish-Style Mussels with Olives

This Spanish-style recipe is great as an appetizer or served as a light dinner with a crisp salad alongside. Serve these mussels with crusty bread for soaking up the tasty cooking juices. Stuffed green olives add to the color and flavor of the dish.

### Serves 4

2 tablespoons olive oil

1 cup chopped onion

4 cloves garlic, chopped

1/2 teaspoon crushed red chile flakes

3 pounds mussels, scrubbed and debearded

1/4 cup medium-dry or dry sherry or white wine

1 cup diced tomato

1/2 cup chopped green olives

Juice of 1 lemon

2 tablespoons chopped fresh parsley

Heat the oil in a large sauté pan over medium-high heat. Add the onion, garlic, and red chile flakes, and cook until the onion is aromatic and slightly tender, 3 to 4 minutes. Add the mussels, tossing so they are evenly coated in the mixture. Pour on the sherry, cover the pan, and steam until the mussels open, 4 to 5 minutes. Discard any mussels that remain closed. Add the tomato, olives, lemon juice, and parsley, and gently stir just to mix. Spoon the mussels onto small individual plates and drizzle the cooking liquids over. Serve immediately.

# Spicy Scallops and Cabbage

Seafood alternatives: Shrimp, Rock Shrimp, Diced Firm Fish Such as Swordfish or Tuna

A good stir-fry has three basic components—a marinade, fresh vegetables, and a well-seasoned sauce. This recipe can be altered to your whim. Substitute oyster sauce or prepared black bean sauce for the chile paste, or green beans for the cabbage. Just make sure you have all of the ingredients ready before you start to cook.

**Serves 4**

³/₄ **pound scallops**

**Marinade**

1 **tablespoon soy sauce**

2 **teaspoons medium dry sherry, shaoxing wine, or chicken stock**

¹/₂ **teaspoon sugar**

¹/₄ **teaspoon salt**

¹/₄ **teaspoon freshly ground black pepper**

1 **teaspoon cornstarch**

Stir together the scallops and the marinade ingredients and let marinate while you are preparing the remaining ingredients.

Mix the sauce ingredients well and set aside.

Heat a wok or large skillet over high heat. Swirl in half of the oil to coat the sides of the pan. Add the ginger, garlic, white part of the green onion, and the chile, and toss and turn in the pan until they are aromatic and lightly colored, but not brown, 5 or 6 seconds. Lift the scallops from the marinade, leaving any liquids in the bowl. Stir-fry the scallops, and toss in the hot pan with a large spoon until they are evenly opaque, but not fully cooked.

½ cup chicken stock or water

1 to 2 tablespoons Sambal Oelek, or hot red chile paste to taste

1 tablespoon cornstarch

1 teaspoon prepared oyster sauce (optional)

1 teaspoon sugar

¼ teaspoon salt

¼ teaspoon freshly ground black pepper

2 to 3 tablespoons peanut oil or vegetable oil

2 teaspoons finely shredded fresh ginger

2 cloves garlic, sliced

2 green onions, thinly sliced, white parts and green parts kept separate

1 small dried red chile, or ¼ teaspoon crushed red chile flakes

6 to 8 cups sliced napa cabbage

¼ cup medium dry sherry, Shaoxing wine, or chicken stock

A few drops of sesame oil

Remove the scallops to a warm platter.

Wipe the wok dry, place over heat, and swirl in the remaining oil. Cook the cabbage, tossing constantly to evenly cook and coat with the oil. When the sizzling starts to subside in about 30 seconds, swirl in the sherry and toss again to cook in the steam. Return the scallops to the pan with the cabbage and toss to mix.

Add the sauce. Cook, tossing occasionally, until the scallops are just cooked through and the sauce has thickened slightly, about 1 minute.

Arrange the stir-fry on a serving platter and drizzle with sesame oil and the remaining green onions. Serve immediately.

# Steamed Penn Cove Mussels
# with Bagna Cauda

Seafood alternatives: Clams, Shrimp, Crab

*Bagna cauda* is a pungent garlic and olive oil fondue. Literally translated as "warm bath," in Italy it is often traditionally served with raw vegetables. But, if you are a seafood lover, it is almost impossible to keep fresh shellfish out of the dip. Plump, fresh Penn Cove Mussels from Whidbey Island are perfect. Serve the mussels with long forks to swirl in the butter sauce, or pour the sauce over the mussels and serve as an entrée. Just make sure you have lots of good bread to mop up the delectable juices.

## Serves 4

1 head garlic

1/2 cup unsalted butter

2 or 3 anchovy fillets, minced

1/4 teaspoon crushed red chile flakes

1/2 cup extra virgin olive oil

1/4 teaspoon salt

1/4 teaspoon freshly ground black pepper

3 pounds mussels, scrubbed and debearded

1/2 cup water or dry white wine

Break the garlic apart. Peel and thinly slice the cloves. Melt the butter in a small saucepan or in the top of a double-boiler over low heat. Add the garlic, anchovies, and chile flakes. Gently cook over low heat until the garlic is very tender, 15 minutes. Remove from the heat and stir in the olive oil. If the anchovies are very salty, you may not need additional salt. Taste and season accordingly. Add pepper. Serve the sauce at the table in a small fondue pot or a heavy dish placed over a candle warmer.

Place the mussels in a large saucepan over medium-high heat, add 1/2 cup of water, and cover. Steam 3 to 4 minutes, or until mussels begin to open. Uncover and remove cooked mussels as they open. Discard any mussels that remain closed. Serve the hot mussels with long seafood forks so your guests can remove the mussel meat and swirl them in the warm *bagna cauda*. Or, pour the sauce over the mussels and serve in bowls with crusty bread. Serve immediately.

# Index

Panfried Soft-Shell Crab with Roasted Garlic
    and Pepper Vinaigrette, 108–9
  in restaurants, 57
  Simple Stir-Fried Crab, 208
  species of, 102–6, 158
crackers
  Snapper in Saltines, 185
  Sole Mornay, 183–84
Craig, Alaska, 173
crappie, 54
crawfish
  as an alternative, 35, 139
  Crawfish Cornbread, 203
Curried Skate with Lentils and Chapatis, 26–27

# D

dashi, 23
DeVlieger, Debra, 71–72
Dilokvilas, Suvisist, 186–90
Dolly Varden, 54
Donaldson, Lauren, 39
Dungeness crab, 104–5
  Dungeness Crab Club Sandwiches, 107
  Mom's Barbecued Crab, 89
  Simple Stir-Fried Crab, 208
Dunn, Jean, 38
Dutch Harbor, Alaska, 136

# E

eel
  Eel Stewed in Red Wine, 128
  life cycle of, 125–26
  preparing, 126
eggs
  Breakfast Fry Up, 68
  Hangtown Strata, 122

Eliot, T. S., 102
Ellena, Alberto, 79
"Emergency" Fried Oysters, 115
Emeril's, 197, 198–99
equipment, 110
Eskimos, 151
Evergreen State College, 98

# F

FDA. *See* Food & Drug Administration
Fennel, Grilled Halibut with Oregano and, 172
fish. *See also* individual species
  appearance of, 7–8, 72
  bones of, 36–39
  coldwater vs. warmwater, 161–63
  determining quality of, 7–9, 70–72
  eyes, 125
  fillets, 8, 65–66
  following your, 124–27
  frozen, 8, 136, 168
  names of, 52–54
  raw, 141–47
  smell of, 8–9, 70–72
  taste of, 9
  texture of, 161–62
  touching, 9
Fish on a Stick, 116
Fish Stock, 133
Floridian seafood, 106
flying fish roe, 127
Food & Drug Administration (FDA), 7, 71–72,
    121, 157, 163
Fowler, Roy, 206
"fresh," meaning of, 58–59, 136
Fritters, Brazilian Shrimp, 77–78
frozen seafood, 8, 136, 168